Race Matters

Cornel West

Race Matters

BEACON PRESS
BOSTON

Beacon Press
25 Beacon Street
Boston, Massachusetts 02108-2892

Beacon Press books are published under the auspices of
the Unitarian Universalist Association of Congregations.

99 98 97 96 95 94 93   8 7 6 5 4 3 2

Text design by Daniel Ochsner

Typeset by Technologies 'N Typography

Earlier versions of some of the chapters in this book appeared in the following
publications: "Learning to Talk of Race," in the *New York Times Magazine*, August 2,
1992; "Nihilism in Black America," in *Dissent*, Spring 1991; "The Pitfalls of Racial
Reasoning," in *Racing Justice, Engendering Power*, edited by Toni Morrison (New York:
Pantheon, 1992); "The Crisis of Black Leadership," in *Z Magazine*, February 1988;
"Demystifying the New Black Conservatism," in *Praxis International*, July 1987;
"Beyond Affirmative Action: Equality and Identity," in *The American Prospect*, Spring
1992; "On Black-Jewish Relations," in *Emerge*, January 1993, and in *Tikkun*,
January/February 1992; "Malcolm X and Black Rage," in *Malcolm X in Our Own
Image*, edited by Joe Wood (New York: St. Martin's Press, 1992).

Library of Congress Cataloging-in-Publication Data

West, Cornel.
    Race matters / Cornel West.
        p.   cm.
    ISBN 0-8070-0918-0
    1. United States—Race relations. I. Title.
    E185.615.W43 1993
    305.8′00973—dc20   92-35170
                    CIP

To my wonderful son CLIFTON LOUIS WEST
who combats daily the hidden injuries of race
with the most potent of weapons—
love of self and others

Contents

Preface

For the sake of one's children, in order to minimize the bill *they* must pay, one must be careful not to take refuge in any delusion—and the value placed on the color of the skin is always and everywhere and forever a delusion. I know that what I am asking is impossible. But in our time, as in every time, the impossible is the least that one can demand—and one is, after all, emboldened by the spectacle of human history in general, and American Negro history in particular, for it testifies to nothing less than the perpetual achievement of the impossible.

. . . And here we are, at the center of the arc, trapped in the gaudiest, most valuable, and most improbable water wheel the world has ever seen. Everything now, we must assume, is in our hands; we have no right to assume otherwise. If we—and now I mean the relatively conscious whites and the relatively conscious blacks, who must, like lovers, insist on, or create, the consciousness of the others—do not falter in our duty now, we may be able, handful that we are, to end the racial nightmare, and achieve our country, and change the history of the world. If we do not now dare everything, the fulfillment of that prophecy, recreated from the Bible in song by a slave, is upon us: GOD GAVE NOAH THE RAINBOW SIGN, NO MORE WATER, THE FIRE NEXT TIME!

JAMES BALDWIN, *The Fire Next Time* (1963)

THIS past September my wife, Elleni, and I made our biweekly trek to New York City from Princeton. I was in good spirits. My morning lecture on the first half of Plato's *Republic* in my European Cultural Studies course had gone well. And my afternoon lecture on W. E. B. Du Bois's *The Souls of Black Folk* in my Afro-American Cultural Studies course had left me exhausted yet exhilarated. Plato's powerful symbolism of Socrates' descent to the great port of Piraeus—the multicultural center of Greek trade and commerce and the stronghold of Athenian democracy—still rang in my ears. And Du Bois's prescient pronouncement—"The problem of the twentieth century is the problem of the color line"—haunted me. In a mysterious way, this classic twosome posed the most fundamental challenges to my basic aim in life: to speak the truth to power with love so that the quality of everyday life for ordinary people is enhanced and white supremacy is stripped of its authority and legitimacy. Plato's profound—yet unpersuasive—critique of Athenian democracy as inevitably corrupted by the ignorance and passions of the masses posed one challenge, and Du Bois's deep analysis of the intransigence of white supremacy in the American democratic experiment posed another.

As we approached Manhattan, my temperature rose, as it always does when I'm in a hurry near the Lincoln Tunnel. How rare it is that I miss the grinding gridlock—no matter the day or hour. But this time I drove right through and attributed my good luck to Elleni. As we entered the city, we pondered whether we would have enough time to stop at Sweetwater's (our favorite place to relax) after our appointments. I dropped my wife off for an appointment on 60th Street between Lexington and Park avenues. I left my car—a rather elegant one—in a safe parking lot and stood on the corner of 60th Street and Park Avenue to catch a taxi. I felt quite relaxed since I had an hour until my next engagement. At 5:00 P.M. I had to meet a photographer who would take the picture for the cover of this book on the roof of an apartment building in East Harlem on 115th Street and 1st Avenue. I waited and waited and waited. After the ninth taxi refused me, my blood began to boil. The tenth taxi refused me and stopped for a kind, well-dressed, smiling female fellow citizen of European descent. As she stepped in the cab, she said, "This is really ridiculous, is it not?"

Ugly racial memories of the past flashed through my mind. Years ago, while driving from New York to teach at Williams College, I was stopped on fake charges of trafficking cocaine. When I told the police officer I was a professor of religion, he replied "Yeh, and I'm the Flying Nun. Let's go, nigger!" I was stopped three times in my first ten days in Princeton for driving too slowly on a residential street with a speed limit of twenty-five miles per hour. (And my son, Clifton, already has similar memories at the tender age of fifteen.) Needless to say, these incidents are dwarfed by those like

Rodney King's beating or the abuse of black targets of the FBI's COINTELPRO efforts in the 1960s and 1970s. Yet the memories cut like a merciless knife at my soul as I waited on that godforsaken corner. Finally I decided to take the subway. I walked three long avenues, arrived late, and had to catch my moral breath as I approached the white male photographer and white female cover designer. I chose not to dwell on this everyday experience of black New Yorkers. And we had a good time talking, posing, and taking pictures.

When I picked up Elleni, I told her of my hour spent on the corner, my tardy arrival, and the expertise and enthusiasm of the photographer and designer. We talked about our fantasy of moving to Addis Ababa, Ethiopia—her home and the site of the most pleasant event of my life. I toyed with the idea of attending the last day of the revival led by the Rev. Jeremiah Wright of Chicago at Rev. Wyatt T. Walker's Canaan Baptist Church of Christ in Harlem. But we settled for Sweetwater's. And the ugly memories faded in the face of soulful music, soulful food, and soulful folk.

As we rode back to Princeton, above the soothing black music of Van Harper's Quiet Storm on WBLS, 107.5 on the radio dial, we talked about what *race* matters have meant to the American past and of how much race *matters* in the American present. And I vowed to be more vigilant and virtuous in my efforts to meet the formidable challenges posed by Plato and Du Bois. For me, it is an urgent question of power and morality; for others, it is an everyday matter of life and death.

Race Matters

Introduction: Race Matters

Since the beginning of the nation, white Americans have suffered from
a deep inner uncertainty as to who they really are. One of the ways
that has been used to simplify the answer has been to seize upon the
presence of black Americans and use them as a marker, a symbol of
limits, a metaphor for the "outsider." Many whites could look at the
social position of blacks and feel that color formed an easy and
reliable gauge for determining to what extent one was or was not
American. Perhaps that is why one of the first epithets that many
European immigrants learned when they got off the boat was the term
"nigger"—it made them feel instantly American. But this is tricky
magic. Despite his racial difference and social status, something
indisputably American about Negroes not only raised doubts about the
white man's value system but aroused the troubling suspicion that
whatever else the true American is, he is also somehow black.

RALPH ELLISON, "What America Would
Be Like without Blacks" (1970)

W HAT happened in Los Angeles in April of 1992 was
neither a race riot nor a class rebellion. Rather, this
monumental upheaval was a multiracial, trans-class, and largely
male display of justified social rage. For all its ugly, xenophobic
resentment, its air of adolescent carnival, and its downright bar-
baric behavior, it signified the sense of powerlessness in American
society. Glib attempts to reduce its meaning to the pathologies of
the black underclass, the criminal actions of hoodlums, or the
political revolt of the oppressed urban masses miss the mark. Of
those arrested, only 36 percent were black, more than a third had
full-time jobs, and most claimed to shun political affiliation. What
we witnessed in Los Angeles was the consequence of a lethal
linkage of economic decline, cultural decay, and political lethargy
in American life. Race was the visible catalyst, not the underlying
cause.

1

Introduction

The meaning of the earthshaking events in Los Angeles is difficult to grasp because most of us remain trapped in the narrow framework of the dominant liberal and conservative views of race in America, which with its worn-out vocabulary leaves us intellectually debilitated, morally disempowered, and personally depressed. The astonishing disappearance of the event from public dialogue is testimony to just how painful and distressing a serious engagement with race is. Our truncated public discussions of race suppress the best of who and what we are as a people because they fail to confront the complexity of the issue in a candid and critical manner. The predictable pitting of liberals against conservatives, Great Society Democrats against self-help Republicans, reinforces intellectual parochialism and political paralysis.

The liberal notion that more government programs can solve racial problems is simplistic—precisely because it focuses *solely* on the economic dimension. And the conservative idea that what is needed is a change in the moral behavior of poor black urban dwellers (especially poor black men, who, they say, should stay married, support their children, and stop committing so much crime) highlights immoral actions while ignoring public responsibility for the immoral circumstances that haunt our fellow citizens.

The common denominator of these views of race is that each still sees black people as a "problem people," in the words of Dorothy I. Height, president of the National Council of Negro Women, rather than as fellow American citizens with problems. Her words echo the poignant "unasked question" of W. E. B. Du Bois, who, in *The Souls of Black Folk* (1903), wrote:

> They approach me in a half-hesitant sort of way, eye me curiously or compassionately, and then instead of saying directly, How does it feel to be a problem? they say, I know an excellent colored man in my town. . . . Do not these Southern outrages make your blood boil? At these I smile, or am interested, or reduce the boiling to a simmer, as the occasion may require. To the real question, How does it feel to be a problem? I answer seldom a word.

Nearly a century later, we confine discussions about race in America to the "problems" black people pose for whites rather than

2

consider what this way of viewing black people reveals about us as a nation.

This paralyzing framework encourages liberals to relieve their guilty consciences by supporting public funds directed at "the problems"; but at the same time, reluctant to exercise principled criticism of black people, liberals deny them the freedom to err. Similarly, conservatives blame the "problems" on black people themselves—and thereby render black social misery invisible or unworthy of public attention.

Hence, for liberals, black people are to be "included" and "integrated" into "our" society and culture, while for conservatives they are to be "well behaved" and "worthy of acceptance" by "our" way of life. Both fail to see that the presence and predicaments of black people are neither additions to nor defections from American life, but rather *constitutive elements of that life.*

To engage in a serious discussion of race in America, we must begin not with the problems of black people but with the flaws of American society—flaws rooted in historic inequalities and longstanding cultural stereotypes. How we set up the terms for discussing racial issues shapes our perception and response to these issues. As long as black people are viewed as a "them," the burden falls on blacks to do all the "cultural" and "moral" work necessary for healthy race relations. The implication is that only certain Americans can define what it means to be American—and the rest must simply "fit in."

The emergence of strong black-nationalist sentiments among blacks, especially among young people, is a revolt against this sense of having to "fit in." The variety of black-nationalist ideologies, from the moderate views of Supreme Court Justice Clarence Thomas in his youth to those of Louis Farrakhan today, rest upon a fundamental truth: white America has been historically weak-willed in ensuring racial justice and has continued to resist fully accepting the humanity of blacks. As long as double standards and differential treatment abound—as long as the rap performer Ice-T is harshly condemned while former Los Angeles Police Chief Daryl F. Gates's antiblack comments are received in polite silence, as long as Dr. Leonard Jeffries's anti-Semitic statements are met with vitriolic outrage while presidential candidate Patrick J. Buchanan's anti-Semitism receives a genteel response—black nationalisms will thrive.

Afrocentrism, a contemporary species of black nationalism, is a gallant yet misguided attempt to define an African identity in a white society perceived to be hostile. It is gallant because it puts black doings and sufferings, not white anxieties and fears, at the center of discussion. It is misguided because—out of fear of cultural hybridization and through silence on the issue of class, retrograde views on black women, gay men, and lesbians, and a reluctance to link race to the common good—it reinforces the narrow discussions about race.

To establish a new framework, we need to begin with a frank acknowledgment of the basic humanness and Americanness of each of us. And we must acknowledge that as a people—*E Pluribus Unum*—we are on a slippery slope toward economic strife, social turmoil, and cultural chaos. If we go down, we go down together. The Los Angeles upheaval forced us to see not only that we are not connected in ways we would like to be but also, in a more profound sense, that this failure to connect binds us even more tightly together. The paradox of race in America is that our common destiny is more pronounced and imperiled precisely when our divisions are deeper. The Civil War and its legacy speak loudly here. And our divisions are growing deeper. Today, eighty-six percent of white suburban Americans live in neighborhoods that are less than 1 percent black, meaning that the prospects for the country depend largely on how its cities fare in the hands of a suburban electorate. There is no escape from our interracial interdependence, yet enforced racial hierarchy dooms us as a nation to collective paranoia and hysteria—the unmaking of any democratic order.

The verdict in the Rodney King case which sparked the incidents in Los Angeles was perceived to be wrong by the vast majority of Americans. But whites have often failed to acknowledge the widespread mistreatment of black people, especially black men, by law enforcement agencies, which helped ignite the spark.

The verdict was merely the occasion for deep-seated rage to come to the surface. This rage is fed by the "silent" depression ravaging the country—in which real weekly wages of all American workers since 1973 have declined nearly 20 percent, while at the same time wealth has been upwardly distributed.

The exodus of stable industrial jobs from urban centers to cheaper labor markets here and abroad, housing policies that have created "chocolate cities and vanilla suburbs" (to use the popular musical artist George Clinton's memorable phrase), white fear of black crime, and the urban influx of poor Spanish-speaking and Asian immigrants—all have helped erode the tax base of American cities just as the federal government has cut its supports and programs. The result is unemployment, hunger, homelessness, and sickness for millions.

And a pervasive spiritual impoverishment grows. The collapse of meaning in life—the eclipse of hope and absence of love of self and others, the breakdown of family and neighborhood bonds—leads to the social deracination and cultural denudement of urban dwellers, especially children. We have created rootless, dangling people with little link to the supportive networks—family, friends, school—that sustain some sense of purpose in life. We have witnessed the collapse of the spiritual communities that in the past helped Americans face despair, disease, and death and that transmit through the generations dignity and decency, excellence and elegance.

The result is lives of what we might call "random nows," of fortuitous and fleeting moments preoccupied with "getting over"—with acquiring pleasure, property, and power by any means necessary. (This is not what Malcolm X meant by this famous phrase.) Post-modern culture is more and more a market culture dominated by gangster mentalities and self-destructive wantonness. This culture engulfs all of us—yet its impact on the disadvantaged is devastating, resulting in extreme violence in everyday life. Sexual violence against women and homicidal assaults by young black men on one another are only the most obvious signs of this empty quest for pleasure, property, and power.

Last, this rage is fueled by a political atmosphere in which images, not ideas, dominate, where politicians spend more time raising money than debating issues. The functions of parties have been displaced by public polls, and politicians behave less as thermostats that determine the climate of opinion than as thermometers registering the public mood. American politics has been rocked by an unleashing of greed among opportunistic public officials—who have followed the lead of their counterparts in the private sphere, where, as of 1989, 1 percent of the population owned 37 percent of the wealth and 10 percent of the population owned 86 percent of the wealth—leading to a profound cynicism and pessimism among the citizenry.

And given the way in which the Republican Party since 1968 has appealed to popular xenophobic images—playing the black, female, and homophobic cards to realign the electorate along race, sex, and sexual-orientation lines—it is no surprise that the notion that we are all part of one garment of destiny is discredited. Appeals to special interests rather than to public interests reinforce this polarization. The Los Angeles upheaval was an expression of utter fragmentation by a powerless citizenry that includes not just the poor but all of us.

WHAT is to be done? How do we capture a new spirit and vision to meet the challenges of the post-industrial city, post-modern culture, and post-party politics?

First, we must admit that the most valuable sources for help, hope, and power consist of ourselves and our common history. As in the ages of Lincoln, Roosevelt, and King, we must look to new frameworks and languages to understand our multilayered crisis and overcome our deep malaise.

Second, we must focus our attention on the public square—the common good that undergirds our national and global destinies. The vitality of any public square ultimately depends on how much we *care* about the quality of our lives together. The neglect of our public infrastructure, for example—our water and sewage systems, bridges, tunnels, highways, subways, and streets—reflects not only our myopic economic policies, which impede productivity, but also the low priority we place on our common life.

The tragic plight of our children clearly reveals our deep disregard for public well-being. About one out of every five children in this country lives in poverty, including one out of every two black children and two out of every five Hispanic children. Most of our children—neglected by overburdened parents and bombarded by the market values of profit-hungry corporations—are ill-equipped to live lives of spiritual and cultural quality. Faced with these facts, how do we expect ever to constitute a vibrant society?

One essential step is some form of large-scale public intervention to ensure access to basic social goods—housing, food, health care, education, child care, and jobs. We must invigorate the common good with a mixture of government, business, and labor that does not follow any existing blueprint. After a period in which the private sphere has been sacralized and the public square gutted, the temptation is to make a fetish of the public square. We need to resist such dogmatic swings.

Last, the major challenge is to meet the need to generate new leadership. The paucity of courageous leaders—so apparent in the response to the events in Los Angeles—requires that we look beyond the same elites and voices that recycle the older frameworks. We need leaders—neither saints nor sparkling television personalities—who can situate themselves within a larger historical narrative of this country and our world, who can grasp the complex dynamics of our peoplehood and imagine a future grounded in the best of our past, yet who are attuned to the frightening obstacles that now perplex us. Our ideals of freedom, democracy, and equality must be invoked to invigorate all of us, especially the landless, propertyless, and luckless. Only a visionary leadership that can motivate "the better angels of our nature," as Lincoln said, and activate possibilities for a freer, more efficient, and stable America—only that leadership deserves cultivation and support.

This new leadership must be grounded in grass-roots organizing that highlights democratic accountability. Whoever *our* leaders will be as we approach the twenty-first century, their challenge will be to help Americans determine whether a genuine multiracial democracy can be created and sustained in an era of global economy and a moment of xenophobic frenzy.

Let us hope and pray that the vast intelligence, imagination, humor, and courage of Americans will not fail us. Either we learn a new language of empathy and compassion, or the fire this time will consume us all.

CHAPTER 1

Nihilism in Black America

> We black folk, our history and our present being, are a mirror
> of all the manifold experiences of America. What we want, what we
> represent, what we endure is what America *is*. If we black folk perish,
> America will perish. If America has forgotten her past, then let her
> look into the mirror of our consciousness and she will see the *living*
> past living in the present, for our memories go back, through our
> black folk of today, through the recollections of our black parents, and
> through the tales of slavery told by our black grandparents, to the
> time when none of us, black or white, lived in this fertile land.
> The differences between black folk and white folk are not blood or
> color, and the ties that bind us are deeper than those that separate us.
> The common road of hope which we all traveled has brought us
> into a stronger kinship than any words, laws, or legal claims.

RICHARD WRIGHT, *12 Million Black Voices* (1941)

RECENT discussions about the plight of African Americans—especially those at the bottom of the social
ladder—tend to divide into two camps. On the one hand, there are
those who highlight the *structural* constraints on the life chances
of black people. Their viewpoint involves a subtle historical and
sociological analysis of slavery, Jim Crowism, job and residential
discrimination, skewed unemployment rates, inadequate health
care, and poor education. On the other hand, there are those who
stress the *behavioral* impediments on black upward mobility. They
focus on the waning of the Protestant ethic—hard work, deferred
gratification, frugality, and responsibility—in much of black America.

Those in the first camp—the liberal structuralists—call for full
employment, health, education, and child-care programs, and
broad affirmative action practices. In short, a new, more sober
version of the best of the New Deal and the Great Society: more
government money, better bureaucrats, and an active citizenry.
Those in the second camp—the conservative behaviorists—promote self-help programs, black business expansion, and non-
preferential job practices. They support vigorous "free market"

11

strategies that depend on fundamental changes in how black people act and live. To put it bluntly, their projects rest largely upon a cultural revival of the Protestant ethic in black America.

Unfortunately, these two camps have nearly suffocated the crucial debate that should be taking place about the prospects for black America. This debate must go far beyond the liberal and conservative positions in three fundamental ways. First, we must acknowledge that structures and behavior are inseparable, that institutions and values go hand in hand. How people act and live are shaped—though in no way dictated or determined—by the larger circumstances in which they find themselves. These circumstances can be changed, their limits attenuated, by positive actions to elevate living conditions.

Second, we should reject the idea that structures are primarily economic and political creatures—an idea that sees culture as an ephemeral set of behavioral attitudes and values. Culture is as much a structure as the economy or politics; it is rooted in institutions such as families, schools, churches, synagogues, mosques, and communication industries (television, radio, video, music). Similarly, the economy and politics are not only influenced by values but also promote particular cultural ideals of the good life and good society.

Third, and most important, we must delve into the depths where neither liberals nor conservatives dare to tread, namely, into the murky waters of despair and dread that now flood the streets of black America. To talk about the depressing statistics of unemployment, infant mortality, incarceration, teenage pregnancy, and violent crime is one thing. But to face up to the monumental eclipse of hope, the unprecedented collapse of meaning, the incredible disregard for human (especially black) life and property in much of black America is something else.

The liberal/conservative discussion conceals the most basic issue now facing black America: *the nihilistic threat to its very existence.* This threat is not simply a matter of relative economic deprivation and political powerlessness—though economic well-being and political clout are requisites for meaningful black progress. It is primarily a question of speaking to the profound sense of psychological depression, personal worthlessness, and social despair so widespread in black America.

The liberal structuralists fail to grapple with this threat for two reasons. First, their focus on structural constraints relates almost exclusively to the economy and politics. They show no understanding of the structural character of culture. Why? Because they tend to view people in egoistic and rationalist terms according to which they are motivated primarily by self-interest and self-preservation. Needless to say, this is partly true about most of us. Yet, people, especially degraded and oppressed people, are also hungry for identity, meaning, and self-worth.

The second reason liberal structuralists overlook the nihilistic threat is a sheer failure of nerve. They hesitate to talk honestly about culture, the realm of meanings and values, because doing so seems to lend itself too readily to conservative conclusions in the narrow way Americans discuss race. If there is a hidden taboo among liberals, it is to resist talking *too much* about values because such discussions remove the focus from structures and especially because they obscure the positive role of government. But this failure by liberals leaves the existential and psychological realities of black people in the lurch. In this way, liberal structuralists neglect the battered identities rampant in black America.

As for the conservative behaviorists, they not only misconstrue the nihilistic threat but inadvertently contribute to it. This is a serious charge, and it rests upon several claims. Conservative behaviorists talk about values and attitudes as if political and economic structures hardly exist. They rarely, if ever, examine the innumerable cases in which black people do act on the Protestant ethic and still remain at the bottom of the social ladder. Instead, they highlight the few instances in which blacks ascend to the top, as if such success is available to all blacks, regardless of circumstances. Such a vulgar rendition of Horatio Alger in blackface may serve as a source of inspiration to some—a kind of model for those already on the right track. But it cannot serve as a substitute for serious historical and social analysis of the predicaments of and prospects for all black people, especially the grossly disadvantaged ones.

Conservative behaviorists also discuss black culture as if acknowledging one's obvious victimization by white supremacist practices (compounded by sexism and class condition) is taboo. They tell black people to see themselves as agents, not victims. And on the surface, this is comforting advice, a nice cliché for downtrodden people. But inspirational slogans cannot substitute for substantive historical and social analysis. While black people have never been simply victims, wallowing in self-pity and begging for white giveaways, they have been—and are—*victimized*. Therefore, to call on black people to be agents makes sense only if we also examine the dynamics of this victimization against which their agency will, in part, be exercised. What is particularly naive and peculiarly vicious about the conservative behavioral outlook is that it tends to deny the lingering effect of black history—a history inseparable from though not reducible to victimization. In this way, crucial and indispensable themes of self-help and personal responsibility are wrenched out of historical context and contemporary circumstances—as if it is all a matter of personal will.

This ahistorical perspective contributes to the nihilistic threat within black America in that it can be used to justify right-wing cutbacks for poor people struggling for decent housing, child care, health care, and education. As I pointed out above, the liberal perspective is deficient in important ways, but even so liberals are right on target in their critique of conservative government cutbacks for services to the poor. These ghastly cutbacks are one cause of the nihilist threat to black America.

THE proper starting point for the crucial debate about the prospects for black America is an examination of the nihilism that increasingly pervades black communities. *Nihilism is to be understood here not as a philosophic doctrine that there are no rational grounds for legitimate standards or authority; it is, far more, the lived experience of coping with a life of horrifying meaninglessness, hopelessness, and (most important) lovelessness.* The frightening result is a numbing detachment from others and a self-destructive disposition toward the world. Life without meaning, hope, and love breeds a coldhearted, mean-spirited outlook that destroys both the individual and others.

Nihilism is not new in black America. The first African encounter with the New World was an encounter with a distinctive form of the Absurd. The initial black struggle against degradation and devaluation in the enslaved circumstances of the New World was, in part, a struggle against nihilism. In fact, the major enemy of black survival in America has been and is neither oppression nor exploitation but rather the nihilistic threat—that is, loss of hope and absence of meaning. For as long as hope remains and meaning is preserved, the possibility of overcoming oppression stays alive. The self-fulfilling prophecy of the nihilistic threat is that without hope there can be no future, that without meaning there can be no struggle.

The genius of our black foremothers and forefathers was to create powerful buffers to ward off the nihilistic threat, to equip black folk with cultural armor to beat back the demons of hopelessness, meaninglessness, and lovelessness. These buffers consisted of cultural structures of meaning and feeling that created and sustained communities; this armor constituted ways of life and struggle that embodied values of service and sacrifice, love and care, discipline and excellence. In other words, traditions for black surviving and thriving under usually adverse New World conditions were major barriers against the nihilistic threat. These traditions consist primarily of black religious and civic institutions that sustained familial and communal networks of support. If cultures are, in part, what human beings create (out of antecedent fragments of other cultures) in order to convince themselves not to commit suicide, then black foremothers and forefathers are to be applauded. In fact, until the early seventies black Americans had the lowest suicide rate in the United States. But now young black people lead the nation in suicides.

What has changed? What went wrong? The bitter irony of integration? The cumulative effects of a genocidal conspiracy? The virtual collapse of rising expectations after the optimistic sixties? None of us fully understands why the cultural structures that once sustained black life in America are no longer able to fend off the

15

nihilistic threat. I believe that two significant reasons why the threat is more powerful now than ever before are the saturation of market forces and market moralities in black life and the present crisis in black leadership. The recent market-driven shattering of black civil society—black families, neighborhoods, schools, churches, mosques—leaves more and more black people vulnerable to daily lives endured with little sense of self and fragile existential moorings.

Black people have always been in America's wilderness in search of a promised land. Yet many black folk now reside in a jungle ruled by a cutthroat market morality devoid of any faith in deliverance or hope for freedom. Contrary to the superficial claims of conservative behaviorists, these jungles are not primarily the result of pathological behavior. Rather, this behavior is the tragic response of a people bereft of resources in confronting the workings of U.S. capitalist society. Saying this is not the same as asserting that individual black people are not responsible for their actions—black murderers and rapists should go to jail. But it must be recognized that the nihilistic threat contributes to criminal behavior. It is a threat that feeds on poverty and shattered cultural institutions and grows more powerful as the armors to ward against it are weakened.

BUT why is this shattering of black civil society occurring? What has led to the weakening of black cultural institutions in asphalt jungles? Corporate market institutions have contributed greatly to their collapse. By corporate market institutions I mean that complex set of interlocking enterprises that have a disproportionate amount of capital, power, and exercise a disproportionate influence on how our society is run and how our culture is shaped. Needless to say, the primary motivation of these institutions is to make profits, and their basic strategy is to convince the public to consume. These institutions have helped create a seductive way of life, a culture of consumption that capitalizes on every opportunity to make money. Market calculations and cost-benefit analyses hold sway in almost every sphere of U.S. society.

The common denominator of these calculations and analyses is usually the provision, expansion, and intensification of *pleasure*. Pleasure is a multivalent term; it means different things to many people. In the American way of life pleasure involves comfort, convenience, and sexual stimulation. Pleasure, so defined, has little to do with the past and views the future as no more than a repetition of a hedonistically driven present. This market morality stigmatizes others as objects for personal pleasure or bodily stimulation. Conservative behaviorists have alleged that traditional morality has been undermined by radical feminists and the cultural radicals of the sixties. But it is clear that corporate market institutions have greatly contributed to undermining traditional morality in order to stay in business and make a profit. The reduction of individuals to objects of pleasure is especially evident in the culture industries—television, radio, video, music—in which gestures of sexual foreplay and orgiastic pleasure flood the marketplace.

Like all Americans, African Americans are influenced greatly by the images of comfort, convenience, machismo, femininity, violence, and sexual stimulation that bombard consumers. These seductive images contribute to the predominance of the market-inspired way of life over all others and thereby edge out nonmarket values—love, care, service to others—handed down by preceding generations. The predominance of this way of life among those living in poverty-ridden conditions, with a limited capacity to ward off self-contempt and self-hatred, results in the possible triumph of the nihilistic threat in black America.

A MAJOR contemporary strategy for holding the nihilistic threat at bay is a direct attack on the sense of worthlessness and self-loathing in black America. This *angst* resembles a kind of collective clinical depression in significant pockets of black America. The eclipse of hope and collapse of meaning in much of black America is linked to the structural dynamics of corporate market institutions that affect all Americans. Under these circumstances black existential *angst* derives from the lived experience of ontological wounds and emotional scars inflicted by white supremacist beliefs and images permeating U.S. society and culture. These

17

beliefs and images attack black intelligence, black ability, black beauty, and black character daily in subtle and not-so-subtle ways. Toni Morrison's novel, *The Bluest Eye,* for example, reveals the devastating effect of pervasive European ideals of beauty on the self-image of young black women. Morrison's exposure of the harmful extent to which these white ideals affect the black self-image is a first step toward rejecting these ideals and overcoming the nihilistic self-loathing they engender in blacks.

The accumulated effect of the black wounds and scars suffered in a white-dominated society is a deep-seated anger, a boiling sense of rage, and a passionate pessimism regarding America's will to justice. Under conditions of slavery and Jim Crow segregation, this anger, rage, and pessimism remained relatively muted because of a well-justified fear of brutal white retaliation. The major breakthroughs of the sixties—more psychically than politically—swept this fear away. Sadly, the combination of the market way of life, poverty-ridden conditions, black existential *angst,* and the lessening of fear of white authorities has directed most of the anger, rage, and despair toward fellow black citizens, especially toward black women who are the most vulnerable in our society and in black communities. Only recently has this nihilistic threat—and its ugly inhumane outlook and actions—surfaced in the larger American society. And its appearance surely reveals one of the many instances of cultural decay in a declining empire.

WHAT is to be done about this nihilistic threat? Is there really any hope, given our shattered civil society, market-driven corporate enterprises, and white supremacism? If one begins with the threat of concrete nihilism, then one must talk about some kind of *politics of conversion.* New models of collective black leadership must promote a version of this politics. Like alcoholism and drug addiction, nihilism is a disease of the soul. It can never be completely cured, and there is always the possibility of relapse. But there is always a chance for conversion—a chance for people to believe that there is hope for the future and a meaning to struggle. This chance rests neither on an agreement about what justice consists of nor on an analysis of how racism, sexism, or class subordination operate. Such arguments and analyses are indispensable. But a politics of conversion requires more. Nihilism is not overcome by arguments or analyses; it is tamed by love and care. Any disease of the soul must be conquered by a turning of one's soul. This turning is done through one's own affirmation of one's worth—an affirmation fueled by the concern of others. A love ethic must be at the center of a politics of conversion.

A love ethic has nothing to do with sentimental feelings or tribal connections. Rather it is a last attempt at generating a sense of agency among a downtrodden people. The best exemplar of this love ethic is depicted on a number of levels in Toni Morrison's great novel *Beloved*. Self-love and love of others are both modes toward increasing self-valuation and encouraging political resistance in one's community. These modes of valuation and resistance are rooted in a subversive memory—the best of one's past without romantic nostalgia—and guided by a universal love ethic. For my purposes here, *Beloved* can be construed as bringing together the loving yet critical affirmation of black humanity found in the best of black nationalist movements, the perennial hope against hope for trans-racial coalition in progressive movements, and the painful struggle for self-affirming sanity in a history in which the nihilistic threat *seems* insurmountable.

The politics of conversion proceeds principally on the local level—in those institutions in civil society still vital enough to promote self-worth and self-affirmation. It surfaces on the state and national levels only when grassroots democratic organizations put forward a collective leadership that has earned the love and respect of and, most important, has proved itself *accountable* to these organizations. This collective leadership must exemplify moral integrity, character, and democratic statesmanship within itself and within its organizations.

Like liberal structuralists, the advocates of a politics of conversion never lose sight of the structural conditions that shape the sufferings and lives of people. Yet, unlike liberal structuralism, the politics of conversion meets the nihilistic threat head-on. Like conservative behaviorism, the politics of conversion openly confronts the self-destructive and inhumane actions of black people.

Unlike conservative behaviorists, the politics of conversion situates these actions within inhumane circumstances (but does not thereby exonerate them). The politics of conversion shuns the limelight—a limelight that solicits status seekers and ingratiates egomaniacs. Instead, it stays on the ground among the toiling everyday people, ushering forth humble freedom fighters—both followers and leaders—who have the audacity to take the nihilistic threat by the neck and turn back its deadly assaults.

CHAPTER 2

The Pitfalls
of Racial Reasoning

Insistence on patriarchal values, on equating black liberation with black men gaining access to male privilege that would enable them to assert power over black women, was one of the most significant forces undermining radical struggle. Thorough critiques of gender would have compelled leaders of black liberation struggles to envision new strategies and to talk about black subjectivity in a visionary manner.

BELL HOOKS, *Yearning: Race, Gender, and Cultural Politics* (1990)

THE most depressing feature of the Clarence Thomas / Anita Hill hearings was neither the mean-spirited attacks of the Republicans nor the spineless silences of the Democrats—both reveal the predictable inability of most white politicians to talk candidly about race and gender. Rather what was most disturbing was the low level of political discussion in black America about these hearings—a crude discourse about race and gender that bespeaks a failure of nerve of black leadership.

This failure of nerve already was manifest in the selection and confirmation process of Clarence Thomas. Bush's choice of Thomas caught most black leaders off guard. Few had the courage to say publicly that this was an act of cynical tokenism concealed by outright lies about Thomas being the most qualified candidate regardless of race. Thomas had an undistinguished record as a student (mere graduation from Yale Law School does not qualify one for the Supreme Court); he left thirteen thousand age discrimination cases dying on the vine for lack of investigation in his turbulent eight years at the EEOC; and his performance during his short fifteen months as an appellate court judge was mediocre. The very fact that no black leader could utter publicly that a black appointee for the Supreme Court was *unqualified* shows how captive they are to white racist stereotypes about black intellectual talent. The point here is not simply that if Thomas were white they would have no trouble shouting this fact from the rooftops. The point is also that their silence reveals that black leaders may entertain the possibility that the racist stereotype may be true. Hence their attempt to cover Thomas's mediocrity with silence. Of

23

course, some privately admit his mediocrity while pointing out the mediocrity of Justice Souter and other members of the Court—as if white mediocrity were a justification of black mediocrity. No double standards here, the argument goes, if a black man is unqualified one can defend and excuse him by appealing to other unqualified white judges. This chimes well with a cynical tokenism of the lowest common denominator—with little concern for the goal of shattering the racist stereotype or for furthering the public interest of the nation. It also renders invisible highly qualified black judges who deserve serious consideration for selection to the Court.

How did much of black leadership get in this bind? Why did so many of them capitulate to Bush's cynical strategy? First, Thomas's claim to racial authenticity—his birth in Jim Crow Georgia, his childhood as the grandson of a black sharecropper, his undeniably black phenotype degraded by racist ideals of beauty, and his gallant black struggle for achievement in racist America. Second, the complex relation of this claim to racial authenticity to the increasing closing-ranks mentality in black America. Escalating black nationalist sentiments—the notion that America's will to racial justice is weak and therefore black people must close ranks for survival in a hostile country—rests principally upon claims to racial authenticity. Third, the way in which black nationalist sentiments promote and encourage black cultural conservatism, especially black patriarchal (and homophobic) power. The idea of black people closing ranks against hostile white Americans reinforces black male power exercised over black women (e.g., to protect, regulate, subordinate, and hence usually, though not always, to use and abuse women) in order to preserve black social order under circumstances of white literal attack and symbolic assault. (This process is discussed in more detail in chapter 7.)

Most black leaders got lost in this thicket of reasoning and hence got caught in a vulgar form of racial reasoning: black authenticity → black closing-ranks mentality → black male subordination of black women in the interests of the black community in a hostile white racist country. Such a line of racial reasoning leads to such questions as: "Is Thomas really black?" "Is he black enough to be defended?" "Is he just black on the outside?" In fact, these kinds of questions were asked, debated, and answered throughout black America in barber shops, beauty salons, living rooms, churches, mosques, and schoolrooms.

Unfortunately, the very framework of racial reasoning was not called into question. Yet as long as racial reasoning regulates black thought and action, Clarence Thomases will continue to haunt black America—as Bush and other conservatives sit back, watch, and prosper. How does one undermine the framework of racial reasoning? By dismantling each pillar slowly and systematically. The fundamental aim of this undermining and dismantling is to replace racial reasoning with moral reasoning, to understand the black freedom struggle not as an affair of skin pigmentation and racial phenotype but rather as a matter of ethical principles and wise politics, and to combat the black nationalist attempt to subordinate the issues and interests of black women by linking mature black self-love and self-respect to egalitarian relations within and outside black communities. The failure of nerve of black leadership is its refusal to undermine and dismantle the framework of racial reasoning.

Let us begin with the claim to racial authenticity—a claim Bush made about Thomas, Thomas made about himself in the hearings, and black nationalists make about themselves. What is black authenticity? Who is really black? First, blackness has no meaning outside of a system of race-conscious people and practices. After centuries of racist degradation, exploitation, and oppression in America, being black means being minimally subject to white supremacist abuse and being part of a rich culture and community that has struggled against such abuse. All people with black skin and African phenotype are subject to potential white supremacist abuse. Hence, all black Americans have some interest in resisting racism—even if their interest is confined solely to themselves as individuals rather than to larger black communities. Yet how this "interest" is defined and how individuals and communities are understood vary. Hence any claim to black authenticity—beyond

25

that of being a potential object of racist abuse and an heir to a grand tradition of black struggle—is contingent on one's political definition of black interest and one's ethical understanding of how this interest relates to individuals and communities in and outside black America. In short, blackness is a political and ethical construct. Appeals to black authenticity ignore this fact; such appeals hide and conceal the political and ethical dimension of blackness. This is why claims to racial authenticity trump political and ethical argument—and why racial reasoning discourages moral reasoning. Every claim to racial authenticity presupposes elaborate conceptions of political and ethical relations of interests, individuals, and communities. Racial reasoning conceals these presuppositions behind a deceptive cloak of racial consensus—yet racial reasoning is seductive because it invokes an undeniable history of racial abuse and racial struggle. This is why Bush's claims to Thomas's black authenticity, Thomas's claims about his own black authenticity, and black nationalist claims about black authenticity all highlight histories of black abuse and black struggle.

But if claims to black authenticity are political and ethical conceptions of the relation of black interests, individuals, and communities, then any attempt to confine black authenticity to black nationalist politics or black male interests warrants suspicion. For example, black leaders failed to highlight the problematic statements Clarence Thomas made about his sister, Emma Mae, regarding her experience with the welfare system. In front of a conservative audience in San Francisco, Thomas implied she was a welfare cheat dependent on state support. Yet, like most black women in American history, Emma Mae is a hard-working person. She was sensitive enough to take care of her sick aunt even though she was unable to work for a short period of time. After she left welfare, she worked two jobs—until 3:00 in the morning! Thomas's statements reveal his own lack of integrity and character. But the failure of black leaders to highlight his statements discloses a conception of black authenticity confined to black male interests, individuals, and communities. In short, the refusal by most black leaders to give weight to the interests of black women was already apparent before Anita Hill appeared on the scene.

The claims to black authenticity that feed on the closing-ranks mentality of black people are dangerous precisely because this closing of ranks is usually done at the expense of black women. It also tends to ignore the divisions of class and sexual orientation in black America—divisions that require attention if *all* black interests, individuals, and communities are to be taken into consideration. Thomas's conservative Republican politics do not promote a closing-ranks mentality; instead Thomas claims black authenticity for self-promotion, to gain power and prestige. All his professional life he has championed individual achievement and race-free standards. Yet when it looked as though the Senate would not confirm his appointment to the Supreme Court, he played the racial card of black victimization and black solidarity at the expense of Anita Hill. Like his sister, Emma Mae, Anita Hill could be used and abused for his own self-interested conception of black authenticity and racial solidarity.

Thomas played this racial card with success—first with appeals to his victimization in Jim Crow Georgia and later to his victimization by a "hi-tech lynching"—primarily because of the deep cultural conservatism in white and black America. In white America, cultural conservatism takes the form of a chronic racism, sexism, and homophobia. Hence, only certain kinds of black people deserve high positions, that is, those who accept the rules of the game played by white America. In black America, cultural conservatism takes the form of a inchoate xenophobia (e.g., against whites, Jews, and Asians), systemic sexism, and homophobia. Like all conservatisms rooted in a quest for order, the pervasive disorder in white and, especially, black America fans and fuels the channeling of rage toward the most vulnerable and degraded members of the community. For white America, this means primarily scapegoating black people, women, gay men, and lesbians. For black America, this means principally attacking black women and black gay men and lesbians. In this way, black nationalist and black male-centered claims to black authenticity reinforce black cultural conservatism. The support of Louis Farrakhan's Nation of Islam for Clarence Thomas—despite Farrakhan's critique of Republican Party racist and conservative policies—highlights this fact. It also shows how racial reasoning leads different and disparate viewpoints in black America to the same dead end—with substantive ethical principles and savvy wise politics left out.

The undermining and dismantling of the framework of racial reasoning—especially the basic notions of black authenticity, closed-ranks mentality, and black cultural conservatism—lead toward a new framework for black thought and practice. This new framework should be a *prophetic* one of moral reasoning with its fundamental ideas of a mature black identity, coalition strategy, and black cultural democracy. Instead of cathartic appeals to black authenticity, a prophetic viewpoint bases mature black self-love and self-respect on the moral quality of black responses to undeniable racist degradation in the American past and present. These responses assume neither a black essence that all black people share nor one black perspective to which all black people should adhere. Rather, a prophetic framework encourages *moral* assessment of the variety of perspectives held by black people and selects those views based on black dignity and decency that eschew putting any group of people or culture on a pedestal or in the gutter. Instead, blackness is understood to be either the perennial possibility of white supremacist abuse or the distinct styles and dominant modes of expression found in black cultures and communities. These styles and modes are diverse—yet they do stand apart from those of other groups (even as they are shaped by and shape those of other groups). And all such styles and modes stand in need of ethical evaluation. Mature black identity results from an acknowledgment of the specific black responses to white supremacist abuses and a moral assessment of these responses such that the humanity of black people does not rest on deifying or demonizing others.

Instead of a closing-ranks mentality, a prophetic framework encourages a coalition strategy that solicits genuine solidarity with those deeply committed to antiracist struggle. This strategy is neither naive nor opportunistic; black suspicion of whites, Latinos, Jews, and Asians runs deep for historical reasons. Yet there are slight though significant antiracist traditions among whites, Asians, and especially Latinos, Jews, and indigenous people that must not be cast aside. Such coalitions are important precisely because they not only enhance the plight of black people but also because they enrich the quality of life in America.

Last, a prophetic framework replaces black cultural conservatism with black cultural democracy. Instead of authoritarian sensibilities that subordinate women or degrade gay men and lesbians, black cultural democracy promotes the equality of black women and men and the humanity of black gay men and lesbians. In short, black cultural democracy rejects the pervasive patriarchy and homophobia in black American life.

If most black leaders had adopted a prophetic framework of moral reasoning rather than a narrow framework of racial reasoning, the debate over the Clarence Thomas / Anita Hill hearings would have proceeded in a quite different manner in black America. For example, both Thomas and Hill would be viewed as two black Republican conservative supporters of some of the most vicious policies to besiege black working and poor communities since Jim and Jane Crow segregation. Both Thomas and Hill supported an unprecedented redistribution of wealth from working people to well-to-do people in the form of regressive taxation, deregulation policies, cutbacks and slowdowns in public service programs, take-backs at the negotiation table between workers and management, and military buildups at the Pentagon. Both Thomas and Hill supported the unleashing of unbridled capitalist market forces on a level never witnessed in the United States before that have devastated black working and poor communities. These market forces took the principal form of unregulated corporative and financial expansion and intense entrepreneurial activity. This tremendous ferment in big and small businesses—including enormous bonanzas in speculation, leverage buyouts and mergers, as well as high levels of corruption and graft—contributed to a new kind of culture of consumption in white and black America. Never before has the seductive market way of life held such sway in nearly every sphere of American life. This market way of life promotes addictions to stimulation and obsessions with comfort and convenience. Addictions and obsessions—centered primarily around bodily pleasures and status rankings—constitute market moralities of various sorts. The common denominator is a rugged and ragged individualism and rapacious hedonism in quest of a perennial "high" in body and mind.

In the hearings, the image of Clarence Thomas that emerged was one of an exemplary hedonist, a consumer of pornography, captive to a stereotypical self-image of the powerful black man who revels in sexual prowess in a racist society. Anita Hill appeared as the exemplary careerist addicted to job promotion and captive to the stereotypical self-image of the sacrificial black woman who suffers silently and alone. There was reason to suspect that Thomas was not telling the whole truth. He was silent about *Roe v. Wade,* his intentions in the antiabortion essay on Lewis Lehrmann, and the contours of his conservative political philosophy. Furthermore, his obdurate stonewalling in regard to his private life was disturbing. There also should be little doubt that Anita Hill's decision to testify was a break from her careerist ambitions. On the one hand, she strikes me as a person of integrity and honesty. On the other hand, she indeed put a premium on job advancement—even at painful personal cost. Yet her speaking out disrupted this pattern of behavior and she found herself supported only by people who opposed the very conservative Republican policies she otherwise championed, namely, progressive feminists, liberals, and some black folk. How strange she must feel being a hero to her former foes. One wonders whether Judge Bork supported her as fervently as she did him a few years ago.

A prophetic framework of moral reasoning would have liberated black leaders from the racial guilt of opposing a black man for the highest court in the land and of the feeling that one had to choose between a black woman and a black man. Like the Black Congressional Caucus (minus one?), black people could have simply opposed Thomas based on qualifications and principle. And one could have chosen between two black right-wing figures based on their sworn testimonies in light of the patterns of their behavior in the recent past. Similarly, black leaders could have avoided being duped by Thomas's desperate and vulgar appeals to racial victimization by a white male Senate committee who handled him gently (no questions about his private life). Like Senator Hollings, who knows racial intimidation when he sees it (given his past experiences with it), black leaders could have seen through the rhetorical charade and called a moral spade a moral spade.

Unfortunately, most black leaders remained caught in a framework of racial reasoning—even when they opposed Thomas and/or supported Hill. Rarely did we have a black leader highlight the moral content of a mature black identity, accent the crucial role of coalition strategy in the struggle for justice, or promote the ideal of black cultural democracy. Instead, the debate evolved around glib formulations of a black "role model" based on mere pigmentation, an atavistic defense of blackness that mirrors the increasing xenophobia in American life, and circled around a silence about the ugly authoritarian practices in black America that range from sexual harassment to indescribable violence against women. Hence a grand opportunity for substantive discussion and struggle over race and gender was missed in black America and the larger society. And black leadership must share some of the blame. As long as black leaders remain caught in a framework of racial reasoning, they will not rise above the manipulative language of Bush and Thomas—just as the state of siege (the death, disease, and destruction) raging in much of black America creates more urban wastelands and combat zones. Where there is no vision, the people perish; where there is no framework of moral reasoning, the people close ranks in a war of all against all. The growing gangsterization of America results in part from a market-driven racial reasoning that links the White House to the ghetto projects. In this sense, George Bush, David Duke, and many ganster rap artists speak the same language from different social locations—only racial reasoning can save us. Yet I hear a cloud of witnesses from afar—Sojourner Truth, Wendell Phillips, Emma Goldman, A. Phillip Randolph, Ella Baker, Myles Horton, Fannie Lou Hamer, Michael Harrington, Abraham Joshua Heschel, Tom Hayden, Harvey Milk, Robert Moses, Barbara Ehrenreich, Martin Luther King, Jr., and many anonymous others who championed the struggle for freedom and justice in a prophetic framework of moral reasoning. They understood that the pitfalls of racial reasoning are too costly in mind, body, and soul—especially for a downtrodden and despised people like black Americans. The best of our leadership recognized this valuable truth—and more must do so in the future if America is to survive with any moral sense.

CHAPTER 3

The Crisis
of Black Leadership

You don't stick a knife in a man's back nine inches and then pull it
out six inches and say you're making progress.

No matter how much respect, no matter how much recognition, whites
show towards me, as far as I'm concerned, as long as it is not shown
to every one of our people in this country, it doesn't exist for me.

MALCOLM X (1964)

THERE has not been a time in the history of black
people in this country when the quantity of politicians
and intellectuals was so great, yet the quality of both groups has
been so low. Just when one would have guessed that black America
was flexing its political and intellectual muscles, *rigor mortis* seems
to have set in. How do we account for the absence of the Frederick
Douglasses, Sojourner Truths, Martin Luther King, Jrs., Malcolm
Xs, and Fannie Lou Hamers in our time? Why hasn't black America produced intellectuals of the caliber of W. E. B. Du Bois, Anna
Cooper, E. Franklin Frazier, Oliver Cox, and Ralph Ellison in the
past few decades?

A serious response to these perplexing questions requires subtle
inquiry into the emergence of the new black middle class—its
content and character, aspirations and anxieties, orientations and
opportunities. Black America has had a variety of different "middle
classes." Free negroes in the pre–Civil War period; educators,
artisans, and shopkeepers during the Reconstruction period; business persons and black college professors in the years of Jim Crow
laws; and prominent athletes, entertainers, and white collar person-
nel after World War II all serve as examples of black middle-class
status prior to the passing of the Civil Rights Bill in 1964 and the
Voting Rights Bill of 1965. As E. Franklin Frazier pointed out in
his classic *Black Bourgeoisie* (1957), these various forms of black
middle-class status never constituted more than 5 percent of African-Americans before the Civil Rights era. In the last two decades,
this percentage jumped to well over 25 percent. Yet this leap in
quantity has not been accompanied by a leap in quality. The
present-day black middle class is not simply different than its

predecessors—it is more deficient and, to put it strongly, more decadent. For the most part, the dominant outlooks and lifestyles of today's black middle class discourage the development of high quality political and intellectual leaders. Needless to say, this holds for the country as a whole. Yet much of what is bad about the United States, that which prevents the cultivation of quality leadership, is accentuated among black middle-class Americans.

THE new black middle class came of age in the 1960s during an unprecedented American economic boom and in the hub of a thriving mass culture. The economic boom made luxury goods and convenient services available to large numbers of hard-working Americans for the first time. American mass culture presented models of the good life principally in terms of conspicuous consumption and hedonistic indulgence. It is important to note that even the intensely political struggles of the sixties presupposed a perennial economic boom and posited models of the good life projected by U.S. mass culture. Long-term financial self-denial and sexual asceticism was never at the center of a political agenda in the sixties.

The civil rights movement permitted significant numbers of black Americans to benefit from the American economic boom—to get a small, yet juicy piece of the expanding American pie. And for most of those who had the education, skills, and ingenuity to get a piece, mass culture (TV, radio, films) dictated what they should do with it—gain peace of mind and pleasure of body from what they could buy. Like any American group achieving contemporary middle-class station for the first time, black entree into the culture of consumption made status an obsession and addiction to stimulation a way of life. For example, well-to-do black parents no longer sent their children to Howard, Morehouse, and Fisk "to serve the race" (though often for indirect self-serving ends), but rather to Harvard, Yale, and Princeton "to get a high-paying job" (for direct selfish reasons).

One reason quality leadership is on the wane in black America is the gross deterioration of personal, familial, and communal relations among African-Americans. These relations—though always fragile and difficult to sustain—constitute a crucial basis for the development of a collective and critical consciousness and a moral commitment to and courageous engagement with causes beyond that of one's self and family. Presently, black communities are in shambles, black families are in decline, and black men and women are in conflict (and sometimes combat). In this way, the new class divisions produced by black inclusion (and exclusion) from the economic boom and the consumerism and hedonism promoted by mass culture have resulted in new kinds of personal turmoil and existential meaninglessness in black America. There are few, if any, communal resources to help black people cope with this situation.

QUALITY leadership is neither the product of one great individual nor the result of odd historical accidents. Rather, it comes from deeply bred traditions and communities that shape and mold talented and gifted persons. Without a vibrant tradition of resistance passed on to new generations, there can be no nurturing of a collective and critical consciousness—only professional conscientiousness survives. Where there is no vital community to hold up precious ethical and religious ideals, there can be no coming to a moral commitment—only personal accomplishment is applauded. Without a credible sense of political struggle, there can be no shouldering of a courageous engagement—only cautious adjustment is undertaken. If you stop to think in this way about the source of leadership, it becomes clear why there is such a lack of quality leadership in black America today. This absence is primarily a symptom of black distance from a vibrant tradition of resistance, from a vital community bonded by its ethical ideals, and from a credible sense of political struggle. Presently, black middle-class life is principally a matter of professional conscientiousness, personal accomplishment, and cautious adjustment.

Black Political Leadership

Black political leadership reveals the tame and genteel face of the black middle class. The black dress suits with white shirts worn by Malcolm X and Martin Luther King, Jr., signified the seriousness of their deep commitment to black freedom, whereas today the expensive tailored suits of black politicians symbolize their personal success and individual achievement. Malcolm and Martin called for the realization that black people are somebodies with which America has to reckon, whereas black politicians tend to turn our attention to *their* somebodiness owing to *their* "making it" in America.

This crude and slightly unfair comparison highlights two distinctive features of black political leaders in the post–Civil Rights era: the relative lack of authentic anger and the relative absence of genuine humility. What stood out most strikingly about Malcolm X, Martin Luther King, Jr., Ella Baker, and Fannie Lou Hamer was that they were almost always visibly upset about the condition of black America. When one saw them speak or heard their voices, they projected on a gut level that the black situation was urgent, in need of immediate attention. One even gets the impression that their own stability and sanity rested on how soon the black predicament could be improved. Malcolm, Martin, Ella, and Fannie were angry about the state of black America, and this anger fueled their boldness and defiance.

In stark contrast, most present-day black political leaders appear too hungry for status to be angry, too eager for acceptance to be bold, too self-invested in advancement to be defiant. And when they do drop their masks and try to get mad (usually in the presence of black audiences), their bold rhetoric is more performance than personal, more play-acting than heartfelt. Malcolm, Martin, Ella, and Fannie made sense of the black plight in a poignant and powerful manner, whereas most contemporary black political leaders' oratory appeals to black people's sense of the sentimental and sensational.

Similarly, Malcolm, Martin, Ella, and Fannie were examples of humility. Yes, even Malcolm's aggressiveness was accompanied by a common touch and humble disposition toward ordinary black people. Humility is the fruit of inner security and wise maturity. To be humble is to be so sure of one's self and one's mission that one can forego calling excessive attention to one's self and status.

And, even more pointedly, to be humble is to revel in the accomplishments or potentials of others—especially those with whom one identifies and to whom one is linked organically. The relative absence of humility in most black political leaders today is a symptom of the status-anxiety and personal insecurity pervasive in black middle-class America. In this context, even a humble vesture is viewed as a cover for some sinister motive or surreptitious ambition.

Present-day black political leaders can be grouped under three types: race-effacing managerial leaders, race-identifying protest leaders, and race-transcending prophetic leaders. The first type is growing rapidly. The Thomas Bradleys and Wilson Goodes of black America have become a model for many black leaders trying to reach a large white constituency and keep a loyal black one. This type survives on sheer political savvy and thrives on personal diplomacy. This kind of candidate is the lesser of two evils in a political situation where the only other electoral choice is a conservative (usually white) politician. Yet this type of leader tends to stunt progressive development and silence the prophetic voices in the black community by casting the practical mainstream as the only game in town.

The second type of black political leader—race-identifying protest leaders—often view themselves in the tradition of Malcolm X, Martin Luther King, Jr., Ella Baker, and Fannie Lou Hamer. Yet they are usually self-deluded. They actually operate much more in the tradition of Booker T. Washington, by confining themselves to the black turf, vowing to protect their leadership status over it, and serving as power brokers with powerful nonblack (usually white economic or political elites, though in Louis Farrakhan's case it may be Libyan elites) to "enhance" this black turf. It is crucial to remember that even in the fifties, Malcolm X's vision and practice were international in scope, and that after 1964 his project was transracial—though grounded in the black turf. King never confined himself to being solely the leader of black America—even though the white press attempted to do so. And Fannie Lou Hamer led the National Welfare Rights Organization, not the Black Welfare Rights Organization. In short, race-identifying protest leaders in the post–Civil Rights era function as figures who white Americans must appease so that the plight of the black poor is overlooked and forgotten. When such leaders move successfully into elected office—as with Marion Barry—they usually become managerial types with large black constituencies, flashy styles, flowery rhetoric, and Booker T. Washington–like patronage operations within the public sphere.

Race-transcending prophetic leaders are rare in contemporary black America. Harold Washington was one. The Jesse Jackson of 1988 was attempting to be another—yet the opportunism of his past weighed heavily on him. To be an elected official and prophetic leader requires personal integrity and political savvy, moral vision and prudential judgment, courageous defiance and organizational patience. The present generation has yet to produce such a figure. We have neither an Adam Clayton Powell, Jr., nor a Ronald Dellums. This void sits like a festering sore at the center of the crisis of black leadership—and the predicament of the disadvantaged in the United States and abroad worsens.

Black Intellectual Leadership

Black intellectual leadership discloses the cynical and ironic face of the black middle class. The Victorian three-piece suit—with a clock and chain in the vest—worn by W. E. B. Du Bois not only represented the age that shaped and molded him; it also dignified his sense of intellectual vocation, a sense of rendering service by means of critical intelligence and moral action. The shabby clothing worn by most black intellectuals these days may be seen as symbolizing their utter marginality behind the walls of academe and their sense of impotence in the wider world of American culture and politics. For Du Bois, the glorious life of the mind was a highly disciplined way of life and an intensely demanding way of struggle that facilitated transit between his study and the streets; whereas present-day black scholars tend to be mere academicians, narrowly confined to specialized disciplines with little sense of the broader life of the mind and hardly any engagement with battles in the streets.

Black intellectuals are affected by the same processes as other American intellectuals, such as the professionalization and specialization of knowledge, the bureaucratization of the academy, the proliferation of arcane jargon in the various disciplines, and the marginalization of humanistic studies. Yet the quality of black intellectual work has suffered more so than that of others. There are two basic reasons why.

First, the academic system of rewards and status, prestige and influence, puts a premium on those few black scholars who imitate the dominant paradigms elevated by fashionable Northeastern seaboard institutions of higher learning. If one is fortunate enough to be a "spook who sits by the door," eavesdrops on the conversation among the prominent and prestigious, and reproduces their jargon in relation to black subject matter, one's academic career is secure. This system not only demoralizes aspiring careerists stuck in the provinces far from the exciting metropolis; it also stifles intellectual creativity, especially among those for whom the dominant paradigms are problematic. Yet the incredible expansion of the Academy in the past few decades—including the enormous federal dollars that support both private and public universities and colleges—has made the Academy a world in itself and a caretaker of nearly all intellectual talent in American society. Therefore, even the critiques of dominant paradigms in the Academy are *academic* ones; that is, they reposition viewpoints and figures within the context of professional politics inside the Academy rather than create linkages between struggles inside and outside of the Academy. In this way, the Academy feeds on critiques of its own paradigms. These critiques simultaneously legitimate the Academy (enhancing its self-image as a promoter of objective inquiry and relentless criticism) and empty out the more political and worldly substance of radical critiques. This is especially so for critiques that focus on the way in which paradigms generated in the Academy help authorize the Academy. In this way, radical critiques, including those by black scholars, are usually disarmed.

Second, many black scholars deliberately distance themselves so far from the mainstream Academy that they have little to sustain them as scholars. American intellectual life has few places or

41

pockets to support serious scholarly work outside of the Academy and foundations—especially for those in the social sciences and humanities. The major intellectual alternatives to the Academy are journalism, self-support communities (Bohemia and feminist groups), or self-supporting writers (such as Gore Vidal, Norman Mailer, or John Updike). Unfortunately, some frustrated and disgusted black intellectuals revert to isolated groups and insulated conversations that reproduce the very mediocrity that led them to reject the Academy. In this way, mediocrity of various forms and in different contexts suffocates much of black intellectual life. So, despite the larger numbers of black scholars relative to the past (though still a small percentage in relation to white scholars), black intellectual life is a rather depressing scene. With few periodicals available for cross-disciplinary exchange, few organs that show interest in this situation, and few magazines that focus on analyses of black culture and its relation to American society, infrastructures for black intellectual activity are feeble.

Like black politicians, black scholars fall into three basic types—race-distancing elitists, race-embracing rebels, and race-transcending prophets. The first type are dominant at the more exclusive universities and colleges. They often view themselves as the "talented tenth" who have a near monopoly on the sophisticated and cultured gaze of what is wrong with black America. They revel in severe denigration of much black behavior yet posit little potential or possibility in Afro-America. At times, their criticism is incisive—yet it often denigrates into a revealing self-hatred. They tend to distance themselves from black America by ironically calling attention to their own cantankerous marginality. They pontificate about standards of excellence, complexity of analysis, and subtlety of inquiry—yet usually spin out mediocre manuscripts, flat establishmentarian analyses, and uncreative inquiry. Even so, they prosper—though often at the cost of minimal intellectual respect by their white colleagues in the Academy. The mean-spirited writings of a fellow progressive like Adolph Reed, Jr., are an example.

The second type of black intellectual, the race-embracing rebels, often view themselves in the tradition of W. E. B. Du Bois. Yet they are usually wrong. In fact, they fall much more into the tradition of those old stereotypical black college professors who thrived on being "big fish in a little pond." That is, race-embracing rebels express their resentment of the white Academy (including its subtle racism) by reproducing similar hierarchies headed by themselves, within a black context. They rightly rebel against the tribal insularity and snobbish civility of the white academy (and the first type of black scholars), yet, unlike Du Bois, their rebellion tends to delimit their literary productivity and sap their intellectual creativity. Hence, rhetoric becomes a substitute for analysis, stimulatory rapping a replacement for serious reading, and uncreative publications an expression of existential catharsis. Much, though not all, of Afrocentric thought fits this bill.

There are few race-transcending prophets on the current black intellectual scene. James Baldwin was one. He was self-taught and self-styled, hence beholden to no white academic patronage system. He was courageous and prolific, a political intellectual when the engaged leftist Amiri Baraka was a petit bourgeois Bohemian poet named Leroi Jones and the former Black Panther Eldridge Cleaver became a right-wing Republican. He was unswerving in his commitment to fusing the life of the mind (including the craft of writing) with the struggle for justice and human dignity regardless of the fashions of the day or the price he had to pay. With the exception of Toni Morrison, the present generation has yet to produce such a figure. We have neither an Oliver Cox nor a St. Claire Drake. This vacuum continues to aggravate the crisis of black leadership—and the plight of the wretched of the earth deteriorates.

What Is to Be Done?

The nihilistic threat to black America is inseparable from a crisis in black leadership. This crisis is threefold. First, at the national level, the courageous yet problematic example of Jesse Jackson looms large. On the one hand, his presidential campaigns based on a progressive multiracial coalition were *the* major left-liberal response to Reagan's conservative policies. For the first time since the last days of Martin Luther King, Jr.—with the grand exception of Harold Washington—the nearly *de facto* segregation in U.S. progressive politics was confronted and surmounted. On the other hand, Jackson's televisual style resists grass-roots organizing and, most important, democratic accountability. His brilliance, energy, and charisma sustain his public visibility—but at the expense of programmatic follow-through. We are approaching the moment in which this style exhausts its progressive potential.

Other national nonelectoral black leaders—like Benjamin Hooks of the NAACP and John Jacobs of the National Urban League—rightly highlight the traditional problems of racial discrimination, racial violence, and slow racial progress. Yet their preoccupation with race—the mandate from their organizations—downplays the crucial class, environmental, patriarchal, and homophobic determinants of black life changes. Black politicians—especially new victors like Mayor David Dinkins of New York City and Governor Douglas Wilder of Virginia—are participants in a larger, lethargic electoral system riddled with decreasing revenues, loss of public confidence, self-perpetuating mediocrity, and pervasive corruption. Like most American elected officials, few black politicians can sidestep these seductive traps. For all of these reasons, black leadership at the national level tends to lack a moral vision that can organize (not just periodically energize), subtle analyses that enlighten (not simply intermittently awaken), and exemplary practices that uplift (not merely convey status that awes) black people.

Second, this relative failure creates vacuums to be filled by bold and defiant black nationalist figures with even narrower visions, one-note racial analyses, and sensationalist practices. Louis Farrakhan, the early Al Sharpton (prior to 1991), and others vigorously attempt to be protest leaders in this myopic mode—a mode often, though not always, reeking of immoral xenophobia. This kind of black leadership is not only symptomatic of black alienation and desperation in a country more and more indifferent or hostile to the quality of life among black working and poor people; it also reinforces the fragmentation of U.S. progressive efforts that could reverse this deplorable plight. In this way, black nationalist leaders often inadvertently contribute to the very impasse they are trying to overcome: inadequate social attention and action to change the plight of America's "invisible people," especially disadvantaged black people.

Third, this crisis of black leadership contributes to political cynicism among black people; it encourages the idea that we cannot really make a difference in changing our society. This cynicism—already promoted by the larger political culture—dampens the fire of engaged *local* activists who have made a difference. These activists are engaged in protracted grass-roots organization in principled coalitions that bring power and pressure to bear on specific issues. And they are people who have little interest in being in the national limelight, such as the Industrial Areas Foundation efforts of BUILD in Baltimore or Harlem initiatives in Manhattan.

Without such activists there can be no progressive politics. Yet state, regional, and national networks are also required for an effective progressive politics. That is why locally based collective (and especially multigendered) models of black leadership are needed. These models must shun the idea of one black national leader; they also should put a premium on critical dialogue and democratic accountability in black organizations.

THE crisis in black leadership can be remedied only if we candidly confront its existence. We need national forums to reflect, discuss, and plan how best to respond. It is neither a matter of a new Messiah figure emerging, nor of another organization appearing on the scene. Rather, it is a matter of grasping the structural and institutional processes that have disfigured, deformed, and devastated black America such that the resources for nurturing collective and critical consciousness, moral commitment, and courageous engagement are vastly underdeveloped. We need serious strategic and tactical thinking about how to create new models of leadership and forge the kind of persons to actualize these models. These models must not only question our silent assumptions about black leadership—such as the notion that black leaders are *always* middle class—but must also force us to interrogate iconic figures of the past. This includes questioning King's sexism and homopho-

45

bia and the relatively undemocratic character of his organization, and examining Malcolm's silence on the vicious role of priestly versions of Islam in the modern world.

But one point is beyond dispute: The time is past for black political and intellectual leaders to pose as *the* voice for black America. Gone are the days when black political leaders jockey for the label "president of black America," or when black intellectuals pose as the "writers of black America." The days of brokering for the black turf—of posing as the Head Negro in Charge (H.N.I.C.)—are over. To be a serious black leader is to be a race-transcending prophet who critiques the powers that be (including the black component of the Establishment) and who puts forward a vision of moral regeneration and political insurgency for the purpose of fundamental social change for all who suffer from socially induced misery. For the moment, we reflect and regroup with a vow that the 1990s will make the 1960s look like a tea party.

CHAPTER 4

Demystifying
the New Black Conservatism

It is, indeed, one of the basic moral blindspots of American conservatism that its intellectual and leadership energy have never been focussed in a proactive way on America's racial-caste legacy. This represents a fundamental moral crisis of modern American conservatism . . . American conservatives typically ignored the authoritarian and violent racial-caste practices and values arrayed against black Americans in southern states where the vast majority of blacks live. On the other hand, American conservatives have, throughout this century, often embraced freedom movements elsewhere in the world—in Europe, Latin America, East Asia—but always firmly resisting a proactive embrace of the black American civil rights movement as a bona fide freedom movement fully worthy of their support. So it is in the shadow of this dismal record of mainstream American conservatism vis-à-vis black Americans' long and arduous quest for equality of status that new black conservatives have emerged.

MARTIN KILSON, "Anatomy of Black
Conservatism" (1992)

THE publication of Thomas Sowell's *Race and Economics* in 1975 marked the rise of a novel phenomenon in the United States: a visible and aggressive black intellectual conservative assault on traditional black liberal ideas. The promotion of conservative perspectives is not new in African-American history. The preeminent black conservative of this century, George S. Schuyler, published a witty and acerbic column in the influential black newspaper *The Pittsburgh Courier* for decades, and his book *Black and Conservative* is a minor classic in African-American letters. Similarly, the reactionary essays (some of which appeared in *Readers' Digest*) and Republican Party allegiance of the most renowned African-American woman of letters, Zora Neale Hurston, are often overlooked by her contemporary feminist and womanist followers. Yet Sowell's book still signified something new—a bid for conservative hegemony in black political and intellectual leadership in the post–Civil Rights era.

This bid, as yet, has been highly unsuccessful though it has generated much attention from the American media, whose interest is most clearly evident in the hoopla surrounding the recent works of Shelby Steele, Stephen Carter, and Stanley Crouch. The new black conservatism is a response to the crisis of liberalism in Afro-America. This crisis, exemplified partly by the rise of Reaganism and the collapse of left politics, has created an intellectual space that conservative voices of various colors now occupy.

In this context, the writings of my friend and fellow Christian Glenn Loury warrant attention in that he attempts to distance himself from mainstream conservatism, while targeting his critiques at black liberalism; that is, he is a neo-conservative who wants to dislodge traditional liberalism among black Americans. In his forthcoming book, *Free at Last*, he puts forward three basic charges against black liberal thinkers. First, he holds that black liberals adhere to a victim-status conception of black people that results in blaming all personal failings of black people on white racism. Second, he claims that black liberals harbor a debilitating loyalty to the race that blinds them to the pathological and dysfunctional aspects of black behavior. Third, Loury argues that black liberals truncate intellectual discourse regarding the plight of poor black people by censoring critical perspectives which air the "dirty linen" of the black community—that is, they dub neo-conservatives like Loury as "Uncle Toms" and thereby fail to take his views seriously in an intellectual manner.

Loury's charges are noteworthy in that the hegemony of black liberalism—especially among black academic and political elites—does impose restraints on the quality and scope of black intellectual exchange. Furthermore, the more vulgar forms of black liberalism, for example, extreme environmentalism, tend to downplay or ignore the personal responsibility of black people regarding their behavior toward one another and others.

Unfortunately, and ironically, Loury deploys the very rhetorical strategies he denounces in his liberal adversaries. For example, he casts black conservatives and neo-conservatives like himself as victims—victims whose own failings to gain a fair hearing and broad following in Afro-America he attributes to a black liberal conspiracy to discredit them in an *ad hominem* manner. Yet surely the black community is not so gullible, manipulable, and downright callous. It may simply be that the real merits of the case put forward by the new black conservatives are unconvincing and unpersuasive.

In addition, Loury's rejection of blind loyalty to the race is laudable, yet he replaces it with a similarly blind loyalty to the nation. In fact, his major criticism of black liberals and left-liberals is that they put the black community out of step with present-day conservative America because they adopt an excessively adversarial stance to the rest of the country. This criticism amounts not to a deepening and enriching of black intellectual exchange but rather to a defense of new kinds of restrictions in the name of a neo-nationalism already rampant in America—a neo-nationalism that smothers and suffocates the larger American intellectual scene. In this way, Loury's neo-conservatism enacts the very "discourse truncation" he claims to be opposing in his foes. His frequent characterizations of left-liberal views as "anachronistic," "discredited," and "idiosyncratic," without putting forth arguments to defend such claims, exemplify this "discourse truncation."

Loury's halfway-house position between the black conservatism of Thomas Sowell and traditional black liberalism is symptomatic of the crisis of purpose and direction among African-American political and intellectual elites. Three fundamental processes in American society and culture since 1973 set the context for grasping this crisis: the eclipse of U.S. economic predominance in the world; the structural transformation of the American economy; and the moral breakdown of communities throughout the country, especially among the black working poor and very poor.

The symbolic event in the decline of American economic hegemony was the oil crisis, which resulted principally from the solidarity of the OPEC nations. Increasing economic competition from Japan, West Germany, and other nations ended an era of unquestioned U.S. economic power. The resultant slump in the American economy undermined the Keynesian foundation of postwar American liberalism, that is, economic growth accompanied by state regulation and intervention on behalf of disadvantaged citizens.

The impact of the economic recession on African-Americans was immense. Not surprisingly, it more deeply affected the black working poor and very poor than the expanding black middle class. Issues of sheer survival loomed large for the former, while the latter continued to seize opportunities in education, business, and politics. Most middle-class blacks consistently supported the emergent black political class—the black officials elected at the national, state, and local levels—primarily to ensure black upward social mobility. But a few began to feel uncomfortable about how their white middle-class peers viewed them. Mobility by means of affirmative action breeds tenuous self-respect and questionable peer acceptance for middle-class blacks. The new black conservatives voiced these feelings in the forms of attacks on affirmative action programs (despite the fact that they had achieved their positions by means of such programs).

The importance of this quest for middle-class respectability based on merit rather than politics cannot be overestimated in the new black conservatism. The need of black conservatives to gain the respect of their white peers deeply shapes certain elements of their conservatism. In this regard, they simply want what most people want, to be judged by the quality of their skills, not the color of their skin. But the black conservatives overlook the fact that affirmative action policies were political responses to the pervasive refusal of most white Americans to judge black Americans on that basis.

The new black conservatives assume that without affirmative action programs, white Americans will make choices on merit rather than on race. Yet they have adduced no evidence for this. Most Americans realize that job-hiring choices are made both on reasons of merit and on personal grounds. And it is this personal dimension that is often influenced by racist perceptions. Therefore the pertinent debate regarding black hiring is never "merit vs. race" but whether hiring decisions will be based on merit, influenced by race-bias against blacks, or on merit, influenced by race-bias, but with special consideration for minorities and women, as mandated by law. In light of actual employment practices, the black conservative rhetoric about race-free hiring criteria (usually coupled with a call for dismantling affirmative action mechanisms) does no more than justify actual practices of racial discrimination.

Black conservative claims about self-respect should not obscure this fact, nor should they be regarded as different from the normal self-doubts and insecurities of new arrivals in the American middle class. It is worth noting that most of the new black conservatives are first-generation middle-class persons, who offer themselves as examples of how well the system works for those willing to sacrifice and work hard. Yet, in familiar American fashion, genuine white peer acceptance still preoccupies—and often escapes—them. In this regard, they are still affected by white racism.

The eclipse of U.S. hegemony in the world is also an important factor for understanding black conservatives' views on foreign policy. Although most of the press attention they receive has to do with their provocative views on domestic issues, I would suggest that the widespread support black conservatives received from conservatives in the Reagan and Bush administrations and Jewish neo-conservatives has much to do with their views on U.S. foreign policies. Though black conservatives rightly call attention to the butchery of bureaucratic elites in Africa, who rule in the name of a variety of ideologies, they reserve most of their energies for supporting U.S. intervention in Central America and the U.S. substantive aid to Israel. Their relative silence regarding the U.S. policy of "constructive engagement" with South Africa is also revealing.

The black conservatives' stance is significant in light of the dramatic shift that has occurred in black America regarding America's role in the world. A consequence of the civil rights movement and the black power ideology of the sixties was a growing identification of black Americans with other oppressed peoples around the world. This has had less to do with a common skin color and more to do with shared social and political experience. Many blacks sympathize with Polish workers and Northern Irish Catholics (despite problematic Polish-black and Irish-black relations in places like Chicago and Boston), and more and more blacks are cognizant of how South Africa oppresses its native peoples, how Chile and South Korea repress their citizens, and how Israel mistreats the Palestinians. In fact, the radical consequences for domestic issues of this growing black international consciousness—usually dubbed anti-Americanism by the vulgar right—frightens the new black conservatives, who find themselves viewed in many black communities as mere apologists for pernicious U.S. foreign policies.

We can further understand the rise of the new black conservatives by highlighting the structural transformation of the U.S. economy. The contraction of the manufacturing sector and the expansion of the service sector of the labor market has narrowed job opportunities for semi-skilled and unskilled workers. Coupled with the decline of industrial jobs, which were a major source of black employment, is the most crucial transformation in the U.S. economy affecting black Americans in the past four decades; this is the mechanization of southern agriculture. Forty years ago, 50 percent of all black teenagers had agricultural jobs, and more than 90 percent of those workers lived in the South. As these jobs disappeared, the black unemployment problem in urban centers mushroomed. The recent deindustrialization of northeastern and midwestern cities has exacerbated this problem. And with the added competition for jobs resulting from the entrance of new immigrants and white women into the labor market, semi-skilled and unskilled black workers have found it increasingly difficult, if not impossible, to find employment. By 1980, 15 percent of all black men between the ages of twenty-five and forty-six reported to the Census Bureau that they had earned nothing whatsoever the previous year. Often the only option for young blacks is military enlistment. (Indeed, the U.S. army is nearly one-third black.)

The new black conservatives have rightly perceived that the black liberal leadership has not addressed these changes in the economy. Obviously, the idea that racial discrimination is the sole cause of the predicament of the black working poor and very poor is specious. And the idea that the courts and government can significantly enhance the plight of blacks by enforcing laws already on the books is even more spurious. White racism, though pernicious and potent, cannot fully explain the socioeconomic position of the majority of black Americans.

The crisis of black liberalism is the result of its failure to put forward a realistic response to the changes in the economy. The new black conservatives have highlighted this crisis by trying to discredit the black liberal leadership, arguing that the NAACP, the National Urban League, the Black Congressional Caucus, and most black elected officials are guided by outdated and ineffective viewpoints. The overriding aim of the new black conservatives is to undermine the position of black liberals and replace them with black Republicans (or even conservative black Democrats), who downplay governmental regulation and stress market mechanisms and success-oriented values in black communities.

Yet the new black conservatives have been unable to convince black Americans that conservative ideology and the policies of the Reagan and Bush administrations are morally acceptable and politically advantageous. The vast depoliticization and electoral disengagement of blacks suggests that they are indeed disenchanted with black liberals and distrustful of American political processes; and a downtrodden and degraded people with limited options may be ready to try any alternative. Nevertheless, black Americans have systematically rejected the arguments of the new black conservatives. This is not because blacks are duped by liberal black politicians nor because blacks worship the Democratic Party. Rather, it is because most blacks conclude that while racial discrimination is not the sole cause of their plight, it certainly is one cause. Thus, most black Americans view the new black conservative assault on the black liberal leadership as a step backward rather than forward. Black liberalism indeed is inadequate, but black conservatism is unacceptable. This negative reaction to black conservatives by most blacks partly explains the relative reluctance of some of the new black conservatives to engage in public debates in the black community, and their contrasting eagerness to do so in the mass media, where a few go as far as to portray themselves as courageous, embattled critics of a black liberal establishment—even while their salaries, honorariums, and travel expenses are payed by well-endowed conservative foundations and corporations.

The new black conservatives have had their most salutary effect on public discourse by highlighting the breakdown of the moral fabric in the country and especially in black working poor and very poor communities. Black organizations like Rev. Jesse Jackson's

PUSH have focused on this issue in the past, but the new black conservatives have been obsessed by it, and thereby have given it national attention. Unfortunately, they view this urgent set of problems in primarily individualistic terms and fail to take seriously the historical background and social context of the current crisis.

The black conservatives claim that the decline of values such as patience, deferred gratification, and self-reliance have resulted in the high crime rates, the increasing number of unwed mothers, and the relatively uncompetitive academic performances of black youth. And certainly these sad realities must be candidly confronted. But nowhere in their writings do the new black conservatives examine the pervasiveness of sexual and military images used by the mass media and deployed by the advertising industry in order to entice and titillate consumers. Black conservatives thus overlook the degree to which market forces of advanced capitalist processes thrive on sexual and military images. Even a neo-liberal like Daniel Bell, in stark contrast to black conservatives, highlights the larger social and cultural forces, for example, consumerism and hedonism, which undermine the Protestant ethic and its concomitant values. Yet Bell also tends to downplay the contribution of American capitalism to this process.

Since the end of the postwar economic boom, certain strategies have been intensified to stimulate consumption, especially strategies aimed at American youth that project sexual activity as instant fulfillment and violence as the locus of machismo identity. This market activity has contributed greatly to the disorientation and confusion of American youth, and those with less education and fewer opportunities bear the brunt of this cultural chaos. Ought we to be surprised that black youths isolated from the labor market, marginalized by decrepit urban schools, devalued by alienating ideals of Euro-American beauty, and targeted by an unprecedented drug invasion exhibit high rates of crime and teenage pregnancy?

My aim is not to provide excuses for black behavior or to absolve blacks of personal responsibility. But when the new black conservatives accent black behavior and responsibility in such a way that the cultural realities of black people are ignored, they are playing a deceptive and dangerous intellectual game with the lives and fortunes of disadvantaged people. We indeed must criticize and condemn immoral acts of black people, but we must do so cognizant of the circumstances into which people are born and under which they live. By overlooking these circumstances, the new black conservatives fall into the trap of blaming black poor people for their predicament. It is imperative to steer a course between the Scylla of environmental determinism and the Charybdis of a blaming-the-victims perspective.

The ideological blinders of the new black conservatives are clearly evident in their attempt to link the moral breakdown of poor black communities to the expansion of the welfare state. For instance, in Sowell's work, the preeminent structural element of political-economic life relevant to the plight of the black poor is the negative role of the state and the positive role of the market. A provocative—and slightly unfair—question to this descendant of slaves sold at the auction block is, Can the market do any wrong?

The new black conservatives claim that transfer payments to the black needy engender a mentality of dependence which undercuts the value of self-reliance and of the solidity of the black poor family. They fail to see that the welfare state was an historic compromise between progressive forces seeking broad subsistence rights and conservative forces arguing for unregulated markets. Therefore it should come as no surprise that the welfare state possesses many flaws. The reinforcing of "dependent mentalities" and the unsettling of the family are two such flaws. But simply to point out these rather obvious shortcomings does not justify cutbacks in the welfare state. In the face of high black unemployment, these cutbacks will not promote self-reliance or strong black families but will only produce even more black cultural disorientation and more devastated black households. This is so because without jobs or incentives to be productive citizens the black poor become even more prone toward criminality, drugs, and alcoholism—the major immediate symptoms of the pervasive black communal and cultural chaos.

On the practical and political level, the only feasible alternative to the welfare state is to create more jobs for poor people—something the private sector is simply uninterested in doing, for it is not in its economic interests to do so. Thus, the market rationality of the private sector relegates poor people to subsistence levels of living and/or unemployment. In the realities of contemporary American politics, to attack the welfare state without linking this attack to a credible jobs program (one that is more than likely supported by the public sector) is to reduce the already limited options of black poor people. To go as far as some new black conservatives have done and support the elimination of nearly every federal benefit program for the nonelderly poor (as put forward in Charles Murray's *Losing Ground* [1984]), is to serve as ideological accomplices to social policies that have genocidal effects on the black poor. The welfare state cannot win a war on poverty, yet it does sustain some boats that would otherwise sink, given the high rate of unemployment.

Yet even effective jobs programs do not fully address the cultural decay and moral disintegration of poor black communities. Like America itself, these communities are in need of cultural revitalization and moral regeneration. There is widespread agreement on this need by all forms of black leadership, but neither black liberals nor the new black conservatives adequately speak to this need.

At present, the major institutional bulwarks against the pervasive meaninglessness and despair in Afro-America are intermediate institutions such as Christian churches, Muslim mosques, and character-building schools. They all are fighting an uphill battle; they cannot totally counter the powerful influence on black people, especially black youths, of the sexual and violent images purveyed by mass media. Yet those intermediate institutions that affirm the humanity of black people, accent their capacities and potentialities, and foster the character and excellence requisite for productive citizenship, are beacons of hope in the midst of the cultural and moral crisis. (My appeal to the positive role of such intermediate associations differs from that of the black conservatives. I view this role as both oppositional to and transformative of prevailing class subordination of American capitalist social relations, whereas they view this role as supportive of such class subordination. In this sense, private voluntary institutions constitute a central terrain of ideological and political contestation for myself and black conservatives—with conflicting aims and goals.)

What then are we to make of the new black conservatives? First, I would suggest that the narrowness of their viewpoints reflects the narrowness of the liberal perspective with which they are obsessed. In fact, a lack of broad vision and subtle analysis, and a refusal to acknowledge the crucial structural features of the black poor situation, characterizes both black liberals and conservatives. The positions of both groups reflects a fight within the black middle-class elite. This parochialism is itself a function of the highly limited alternatives available in contemporary American politics.

Second, the emergence of the new black conservatives signifies a healthy development to the degree that it calls attention to the failures of black liberalism and thereby encourages black politicians and activists to entertain more progressive solutions to the larger problems of social injustice and class inequality. Finally, more visible attacks of the new black conservatives on the black liberal leadership regarding U.S. foreign policy may force black intellectual exchange to focus on the relation of the plight of the Third World to that of poor black (brown, red, yellow, and white) people. Given the rapacious pro-Americanism in foreign affairs in American intellectual life, this focus would be salutary.

Perhaps the widening of the split between black liberal elites and black conservative critics will lead to a more principled and passionate political discourse in and about black America. Such a discourse would promote more rational debates among conservative, liberal, and leftist voices concerning strategies to enhance the life-chances of the black poor. The few valuable insights of the new black conservatives can be incorporated into a broader progressive perspective that utterly rejects their unwarranted conclusions and repugnant policies. I suspect that such a dialogue would unmask the new black conservatives as renegades from and critics of a moribund black liberalism who have seen some of the limits of this liberalism, but are themselves unable and unwilling to move beyond it. Hence, the new black conservatives settle for earlier historic versions of classical liberalism in a postliberal society and postmodern culture.

CHAPTER 5

Beyond Affirmative Action:
Equality and Identity

Institutionalized rejection of *difference* is an absolute necessity in a profit economy which needs outsiders as surplus people. As members of such an economy, we have *all* been programmed to respond to the human differences between us with fear and loathing and to handle that difference in one of three ways: ignore it, and if that is not possible, copy it if we think it is dominant, or destroy it if we think it is subordinate. But we have no patterns for relating across our human differences as equals. As a result, those differences have been misnamed and misused in the service of separation and confusion.

AUDRE LORDE, *Sister Outsider* (1984)

THE fundamental crisis in black America is twofold: too much poverty and too little self-love. The urgent problem of black poverty is primarily due to the distribution of wealth, power, and income—a distribution influenced by the racial caste system that denied opportunities to most "qualified" black people until two decades ago.

The historic role of American progressives is to promote redistributive measures that enhance the standard of living and quality of life for the have-nots and have-too-littles. Affirmative action was one such redistributive measure that surfaced in the heat of battle in the 1960s among those fighting for racial equality. Like earlier *de facto* affirmative action measures in the American past—contracts, jobs, and loans to select immigrants granted by political machines; subsidies to certain farmers; FHA mortgage loans to specific home buyers; or GI Bill benefits to particular courageous Americans—recent efforts to broaden access to America's prosperity have been based upon preferential policies. Unfortunately, these policies always benefit middle-class Americans disproportionately. The political power of big business in big government circumscribes redistributive measures and thereby tilts these measures away from the have-nots and have-too-littles.

Every redistributive measure is a compromise with and concession from the caretakers of American prosperity—that is, big business and big government. Affirmative action was one such compromise and concession achieved after the protracted struggle of

63

American progressives and liberals in the courts and in the streets. Visionary progressives always push for substantive redistributive measures that make opportunities available to the have-nots and have-too-littles, such as more federal support to small farmers, or more FHA mortgage loans to urban dwellers as well as suburban home buyers. Yet in the American political system, where the powers that be turn a skeptical eye toward any program aimed at economic redistribution, progressives must secure whatever redistributive measures they can, ensure their enforcement, then extend their benefits if possible.

If I had been old enough to join the fight for racial equality in the courts, the legislatures, and the board rooms in the 1960s (I *was* old enough to be in the streets), I would have favored—as I do now—a class-based affirmative action in principle. Yet in the heat of battle in American politics, a redistributive measure in principle with no power and pressure behind it means no redistributive measure at all. The prevailing discriminatory practices during the sixties, whose targets were working people, women, and people of color, were atrocious. Thus, an *enforceable* race-based—and later gender-based—affirmative action policy was the best possible compromise and concession.

Progressives should view affirmative action as neither a major solution to poverty nor a sufficient means to equality. We should see it as primarily playing a negative role—namely, to ensure that discriminatory practices against women and people of color are abated. Given the history of this country, it is a virtual certainty that without affirmative action racial and sexual discrimination would return with a vengeance. Even if affirmative action fails significantly to reduce black poverty or contributes to the persistence of racist perceptions in the workplace, without affirmative action black access to America's prosperity would be even more difficult to obtain and racism in the workplace would persist anyway.

This claim is not based on any cynicism toward my white fellow citizens; rather, it rests upon America's historically weak will toward racial justice and substantive redistributive measures. This is why an attack on affirmative action is an attack on redistributive efforts by progressives unless there is a real possibility of enacting and enforcing a more wide-reaching class-based affirmative action policy.

In American politics, progressives must not only cling to redistributive ideals, but must also fight for those policies that—out of compromise and concession—imperfectly conform to those ideals. Liberals who give only lip service to these ideals, trash the policies in the name of *realpolitik,* or reject the policies as they perceive a shift in the racial bellwether give up precious ground too easily. And they do so even as the sand is disappearing under our feet on such issues as regressive taxation, layoffs or takebacks from workers, and cutbacks in health and child care.

Affirmative action is not the most important issue for black progress in America, but it is part of a redistributive chain that must be strengthened if we are to confront and eliminate black poverty. If there were social democratic redistributive measures that wiped out black poverty, and if racial and sexual discrimination could be abated through the good will and meritorious judgments of those in power, affirmative action would be unnecessary. Although many of my liberal and progressive citizens view affirmative action as a redistributive measure whose time is over or whose life is no longer worth preserving, I question their view because of the persistence of discriminatory practices that increase black social misery, and the warranted suspicion that good will and fair judgment among the powerful does not loom as large toward women and people of color.

IF the elimination of black poverty is a necessary condition of substantive black progress, then the affirmation of black humanity, especially among black people themselves, is a sufficient condition of such progress. Such affirmation speaks to the existential issues of what it means to be a degraded African (man, woman, gay, lesbian, child) in a racist society. How does one affirm oneself without reenacting negative black stereotypes or overreacting to white supremacist ideals?

The difficult and delicate quest for black identity is integral to any talk about racial equality. Yet it is not solely a political or economic matter. The quest for black identity involves self-respect and self-regard, realms inseparable from, yet not identical to, political power and economic status. The flagrant self-loathing among black middle-class professionals bears witness to this painful process. Unfortunately, black conservatives focus on the issue of self-respect as if it were the one key that would open all doors to black progress. They illustrate the fallacy of trying to open all doors with one key: they wind up closing their eyes to all doors except the one the key fits.

Progressives, for our part, must take seriously the quest for self-respect, even as we train our eye on the institutional causes of black social misery. The issues of black identity—both black self-love and self-contempt—sit alongside black poverty as realities to confront and transform. The uncritical acceptance of self-degrading ideals, that call into question black intelligence, possibility, and beauty not only compounds black social misery but also paralyzes black middle-class efforts to defend broad redistributive measures.

This paralysis takes two forms: black bourgeois preoccupation with white peer approval and black nationalist obsession with white racism.

The first form of paralysis tends to yield a navel-gazing posture that conflates the identity crisis of the black middle class with the state of siege raging in black working-poor and very poor communities. That unidimensional view obscures the need for redistributive measures that significantly affect the majority of blacks, who are working people on the edge of poverty.

The second form of paralysis precludes any meaningful coalition with white progressives because of an undeniable white racist legacy of the modern Western world. The anger this truth engenders impedes any effective way of responding to the crisis in black America. Broad redistributive measures require principled coalitions, including multiracial alliances. Without such measures, black America's sufferings deepen. White racism indeed contributes to this suffering. Yet an obsession with white racism often comes at the expense of more broadly based alliances to affect social change and borders on a tribal mentality. The more xenophobic versions of this viewpoint simply mirror the white supremacist ideals we are opposing and preclude any movement toward redistributive goals.

How one defines oneself influences what analytical weight one gives to black poverty. Any progressive discussion about the future of racial equality must speak to black poverty and black identity. My views on the necessity and limits of affirmative action in the present moment are informed by how substantive redistributive measures and human affirmative efforts can be best defended and expanded.

CHAPTER 6

On Black-Jewish Relations

For if there are no waving flags and marching songs at the barricades as Walter marches out with his little battalion, it is not because the battle lacks nobility. On the contrary, he has picked up in his way, still imperfect and wobbly in his small view of human destiny, what I believe Arthur Miller once called "the golden thread of history." He becomes, in spite of those who are too intrigued with despair and hatred of man to see it, King Oedipus refusing to tear out his eyes, but attacking the Oracle instead. He is that last Jewish patriot manning his rifle at Warsaw; he is that young girl who swam into sharks to save a friend a few weeks ago; he is Anne Frank, still believing in people; he is the nine small heroes of Little Rock; he is Michelangelo creating David and Beethoven bursting forth with the Ninth Symphony. He is all those things because he has finally reached out in his tiny moment and caught that sweet essence which is human dignity, and it shines like the old star-touched dream that it is in his eyes.

LORRAINE HANSBERRY, "An Author's
Reflections: Walter Lee Younger,
Willy Loman and He Who Must Live" (1959)

R ECENT debates on the state of black-Jewish relations have generated more heat than light. Instead of critical dialogue and respectful exchange, we have witnessed several bouts of vulgar name-calling and self-righteous finger-pointing. Battles conducted on the editorial pages, like the one between Henry Louis Gates, Jr., the eminent Harvard professor, and John Henrik Clarke, the distinguished pan-African scholar, in the *New York Times* and the *City Sun*, respectively, do not take us very far in understanding black-Jewish relations.

Black anti-Semitism and Jewish antiblack racism are real, and both are as profoundly American as cherry pie. There was no *golden age* in which blacks and Jews were free of tension and friction. Yet there was a *better* age when the common histories of oppression and degradation of both groups served as a springboard for genuine empathy and principled alliances. Since the late sixties, black-Jewish relations have reached a nadir. Why is this so?

In order to account for this sad state of affairs we must begin to unearth the truth behind each group's perceptions of the other (and

71

of itself). For example, few blacks recognize and acknowledge one fundamental fact of Jewish history: a profound hatred of Jews sits at the center of medieval and modern European cultures. Jewish persecutions under the Byzantines, Jewish massacres during the Crusades, Jewish expulsions in England (1290), France (1306), Spain (1492), Portugal (1497), Frankfurt (1614), and Vienna (1670), and Jewish pogroms in the Ukraine (1648, 1768), Odessa (1871), and throughout Russia—especially after 1881 culminating in Kishinev (1903)—constitute the vast historical backdrop to current Jewish preoccupations with self-reliance and the Jewish anxiety of group death. Needless to say, the Nazi attempt at Judeocide in the 1930s and 1940s reinforced this preoccupation and anxiety.

The European hatred of Jews rests on religious and social grounds—Christian myths of Jews as Christ-killers and resentment over the disproportionate presence of Jews in certain commercial occupations. The religious bigotry feeds on stereotypes of Jews as villainous transgressors of the sacred; the social bigotry, on alleged Jewish conspiratorial schemes for power and control. Ironically, the founding of the state of Israel—the triumph of the quest for modern Jewish self-determination—came about less from Jewish power and more from the consensus of the two superpowers, the United States and USSR, to secure a homeland for a despised and degraded people after Hitler's genocidal attempt.

The history of Jews in America for the most part flies in the face of this tragic Jewish past. The majority of Jewish immigrants arrived in America around the turn of the century (1881–1924). They brought a strong heritage that put a premium on what had ensured their survival and identity—institutional autonomy, rabbinical learning, and business zeal. Like other European immigrants, Jews for the most part became complicitous with the American racial caste system. Even in "Christian" America with its formidable anti-Semitic barriers, and despite a rich progressive tradition that made Jews more likely than other immigrants to feel compassion for oppressed blacks, large numbers of Jews tried to procure a foothold in America by falling in step with the widespread perpetuation of antiblack stereotypes and the garnering of white-skin privilege benefits available to nonblack Americans. It goes without saying that a profound hatred of African people (as seen in slavery, lynching, segregation, and second-class citizenship) sits at the center of American civilization.

The period of genuine empathy and principled alliances between Jews and blacks (1910–67) constitutes a major pillar of American progressive politics in this century. These supportive links begin with W. E. B. Du Bois's *The Crisis* and Abraham Cahan's *Jewish Daily Forward* and are seen clearly between Jewish leftists and A. Philip Randolph's numerous organizations, between Elliot Cohen's *Commentary* and the early career of James Baldwin, between prophets like Abraham Joshua Heschel and Martin Luther King, Jr., or between the disproportionately Jewish Students for a Democratic Society (SDS) and the Student Non-Violent Coordinating Committee (SNCC). Presently, this inspiring period of black-Jewish cooperation is often downplayed by blacks and romanticized by Jews. It is downplayed by blacks because they focus on the astonishingly rapid entree of most Jews into the middle and upper middle classes during this brief period—an entree that has spawned both an intense conflict with the more slowly growing black middle class and a social resentment from a quickly growing black impoverished class. Jews, on the other hand, tend to romanticize this period because their present status as upper middle dogs and some top dogs in American society unsettles their historic self-image as progressives with a compassion for the underdog.

In the present era, blacks and Jews are in contention over two major issues. The first is the question of what constitutes the most effective means for black progress in America. With over half of all black professionals and managers being employed in the public sphere, and those in the private sphere often gaining entree owing to regulatory checks by the EEOC, attacks by some Jews on affirmative action are perceived as assaults on black livelihood. And since a disproportionate percentage of poor blacks depend on government support to survive, attempts to dismantle public programs are viewed by blacks as opposition to black survival. Visible Jewish resistance to affirmative action and government spending on social programs pits some Jews against black progress. This opposition, though not as strong as that of other groups in the country, is all the more visible to black people because of past Jewish support for black progress. It also seems to reek of naked group interest, as well as a willingness to abandon compassion for the underdogs of American society.

The second major area of contention concerns the meaning and practice of Zionism as embodied in the state of Israel. Without a sympathetic understanding of the deep historic sources of Jewish fears and anxieties about group survival, blacks will not grasp the visceral attachment of most Jews to Israel. Similarly, without a candid acknowledgement of blacks' status as permanent underdogs in American society, Jews will not comprehend what the symbolic predicament and literal plight of Palestinians in Israel means to blacks. Jews rightly point out that the atrocities of Africa elites on oppressed Africans in Kenya, Uganda, and Ethiopia are just as bad or worse than those perpetrated on Palestinians by Israeli elites. Some also point out—rightly—that deals and treaties between Israel and South Africa are not so radically different from those between some black African, Latin American, and Asian countries and South Africa. Still, these and other Jewish charges of black double standards with regard to Israel do not take us to the heart of the matter. Blacks often perceive the Jewish defense of the state of Israel as a second instance of naked group interest, and, again, an abandonment of substantive moral deliberation. At the same time, Jews tend to view black critiques of Israel as black rejection of the Jewish right to group survival, and hence as a betrayal of the precondition for a black-Jewish alliance. What is at stake here is not simply black-Jewish relations, but, more importantly, the *moral content* of Jewish and black identities and of their political consequences.

The ascendance of the conservative Likud party in Israel in 1977 and the visibility of narrow black nationalist voices in the eighties helped solidify this impasse. When mainstream American Jewish organizations supported the inhumane policies of Begin and Shamir, they tipped their hats toward cold-hearted interest group calculations. When black nationalist spokesmen like Farrakhan and Jeffries excessively targeted Jewish power as subordinating black and brown peoples they played the same mean-spirited game. In turning their heads from the ugly truth of Palestinian subjugation, and in refusing to admit the falsity of the alleged Jewish conspiracies, both sides failed to define the *moral* character of their Jewish and black identities.

The present impasse in black-Jewish relations will be overcome only when self-critical exchanges take place within and across black and Jewish communities not simply about their own group interest but also, and, more importantly, about what being black or Jewish mean in *ethical terms.* This kind of reflection should not be so naive as to ignore group interest, but it should take us to a higher moral ground where serious discussions about democracy and justice determine how we define ourselves and our politics and help us formulate strategies and tactics to sidestep the traps of tribalism and chauvinism.

The vicious murder of Yankel Rosenbaum in Crown Heights in the summer of 1991 bore chilling testimony to a growing black anti-Semitism in this country. Although this particular form of xenophobia from below does not have the same institutional power of those racisms that afflict their victims from above, it certainly deserves the same moral condemnation. Furthermore, the very *ethical* character of the black freedom struggle largely depends on the open condemnation by its spokespersons of *any* racist attitude or action.

In our present moment, when a neo-Nazi like David Duke can win 55 percent of the white vote (and 69 percent of the white "born-again" Protestant vote) in Louisiana, it may seem misguided to highlight anti-Semitic behavior of black people—the exemplary targets of racial hatred in America. Yet I suggest that this focus is crucial precisely because we black folk have been in the forefront of the struggle against American racism. If these efforts fall prey to anti-Semitism, then the principled attempt to combat racism forfeits much of its moral credibility—and we all lose. To put it bluntly, if the black freedom struggle becomes simply a power-driven war of all against all that pits xenophobia from below against racism from above, then David Duke's project is the wave of the future—and a racial apocalypse awaits us. Despite Duke's resounding defeat, we witness increasing racial and sexual violence, coupled with growing economic deprivation, that together provide the raw ingredients for such a frightening future.

Black people have searched desperately for allies in the struggle against racism—and have found Jews to be disproportionately represented in the ranks of that struggle. The desperation that sometimes informs the antiracist struggle arises out of two conflicting historical forces: America's historically weak will to racial justice *and* an all-inclusive moral vision of freedom and justice for all. Escalating black anti-Semitism is a symptom of this desperation gone sour; it is the bitter fruit of a profound self-destructive impulse, nurtured on the vines of hopelessness and concealed by empty gestures of black unity. The images of black activists yelling "Where is Hitler when we need him?" and "Heil Hitler," juxtaposed with those of David Duke celebrating Hitler's birthday, seem to feed a single fire of intolerance, burning on both ends of the American candle, that threatens to consume us all.

BLACK anti-Semitism rests on three basic pillars. First, it is a species of anti-whitism. Jewish complicity in American racism—even though it is less extensive than the complicity of other white Americans—reinforces black perceptions that Jews are identical to any other group benefitting from white-skin privileges in racist America. This view denies the actual history and treatment of Jews. And the particular interactions of Jews and black people in the hierarchies of business and education cast Jews as the public face of oppression for the black community, and thus lend evidence to this mistaken view of Jews as any other white folk.

Second, black anti-Semitism is a result of higher expectations some black folk have of Jews. This perspective holds Jews to a moral standard different from that extended to other white ethnic groups, principally owing to the ugly history of anti-Semitism in the world, especially in Europe and the Middle East. Such double standards assume that Jews and blacks are "natural" allies, since both groups have suffered chronic degradation and oppression at the hands of racial and ethnic majorities. So when Jewish neoconservatism gains a high public profile at a time when black people are more and more vulnerable, the charge of "betrayal" surfaces among black folk who feel let down. Such utterances resonate strongly in a black Protestant culture that has inherited many stock Christian anti-Semitic narratives of Jews as Christ-killers. These infamous narratives historically have had less weight in the black community, in stark contrast to the more obdurate white Christian varieties of anti-Semitism. Yet in moments of desperation in the black community, they tend to reemerge, charged with the rhetoric of Jewish betrayal.

Third, black anti-Semitism is a form of underdog resentment and envy, directed at another underdog who has "made it" in American society. The remarkable upward mobility of American Jews—rooted chiefly in a history and culture that places a premium on higher education and self-organization—easily lends itself to myths of Jewish unity and homogeneity that have gained currency among other groups, especially among relatively unorganized groups like black Americans. The high visibility of Jews in the upper reaches of the academy, journalism, the entertainment industry, and the professions—though less so percentage-wise in corporate America and national political office—is viewed less as a result of hard work and success fairly won, and more as a matter of favoritism and nepotism among Jews. Ironically, calls for black solidarity and achievement are often modeled on myths of Jewish unity—as both groups respond to American xenophobia and racism. But in times such as these, some blacks view Jews as obstacles rather than allies in the struggle for racial justice.

These three elements of black anti-Semitism—which also characterize the outlooks of some other ethnic groups in America—have a long history among black people. Yet the recent upsurge of black anti-Semitism exploits two other prominent features of the political landscape identified with the American Jewish establishment: the military status of Israel in the Middle East (especially in its enforcement of the occupation of the West Bank and Gaza); and the visible *conservative* Jewish opposition to what is perceived to be a major means of black progress, namely, affirmative action. Of course, principled critiques of U.S. foreign policy in the Middle East, of Israeli denigration of Palestinians, or attacks on affirmative action *transcend* anti-Semitic sensibilities. Yet vulgar critiques do not—and often are shot through with such sensibilities, in white and black America alike. These vulgar critiques—usually based on sheer ignorance and a misinformed thirst for vengeance—add an aggressive edge to black anti-Semitism. And in the rhetoric of a Louis Farrakhan or a Leonard Jeffries, whose audiences rightly hunger for black self-respect and oppose black degradation, these critiques misdirect progressive black energies arrayed against unaccountable corporate power and antiblack racism, steering them instead *toward* Jewish elites and antiblack conspiracies in Jewish America. This displacement is disturbing not only because it is analytically and morally wrong; it also discourages any effective alliances across races.

The rhetoric of Farrakhan and Jeffries feeds on an undeniable history of black denigration at the hands of Americans of every ethnic and religious group. The delicate issues of black self-love and black self-contempt are then viewed in terms of white putdown and Jewish conspiracy. The precious quest for black self-esteem is reduced to immature and cathartic gestures that bespeak an excessive obsession with whites and Jews. There can be no healthy conception of black humanity based on such obsessions. The best of black culture, as manifested, for example, in jazz or the prophetic black church, refuses to put whites or Jews on a pedestal or in the gutter. Rather, black humanity is affirmed alongside that of others, even when those others have at times dehumanized blacks. To put it bluntly, when black humanity is taken for granted and not made to prove itself in white culture, whites, Jews, and others are not that important; they are simply human beings, just like black people. If the best of black culture wanes in the face of black anti-Semitism, black people will become even more isolated as a community and the black freedom struggle will be tarred with the brush of immorality.

For example, most Americans wrongly believe that the black community has been silent in the face of Yankel Rosenbaum's murder. This perception exists because the moral voices in black America have been either ignored or drowned out by the more sensationalist and xenophobic ones. The major New York City newspapers and periodicals seem to have little interest in making known to the public the moral condemnations voiced by Reverend Gary Simpson of Concord Baptist Church in Brooklyn (with ten thousand black members), Reverend James Forbes of Riverside Church (with three thousand members), Reverend Carolyn Knight of Philadelphia Baptist Church in Harlem, Reverend Susan Johnson of Mariners Baptist Church in Manhattan, Reverend Mark Taylor of the Church of the Open Door in Brooklyn, Reverend Victor Hall of Calvary Baptist Church in Queens, and many more. Black anti-Semitism is not caused by media hype—yet it does sell more newspapers and turn our attention away from those black prophetic energies that give us some hope.

My fundamental premise is that the black freedom struggle is the major buffer between the David Dukes of America and the hope for a future in which we can begin to take justice and freedom for all seriously. Black anti-Semitism—along with its concomitant xenophobias, such as patriarchal and homophobic prejudices— weakens this buffer. In the process, it plays into the hands of the old-style racists, who appeal to the worst of our fellow citizens amid the silent depression that plagues the majority of Americans. Without some redistribution of wealth and power, downward mobility and debilitating poverty will continue to drive people into desperate channels. And without principled opposition to xenophobias from above *and* below, these desperate channels will produce a cold-hearted and mean-spirited America no longer worth fighting for or living in.

CHAPTER 7

Black Sexuality:
The Taboo Subject

"Here," she said, "in this here place, we flesh; flesh that weeps, laughs; flesh that dances on bare feet in grass. Love it. Love it hard. Yonder they do not love your flesh. They despise it. They don't love your eyes; they'd just as soon pick em out. No more do they love the skin on your back. Yonder they flay it. And O my people they do not love your hands. Those they only use, tie, bind, chop off and leave empty. Love your hands! Love them. Raise them up and kiss them. Touch others with them, pat them together, stroke them on your face 'cause they don't love that either. *You* got to love it, *You!* . . . This is flesh I'm talking about here. Flesh that needs to be loved."

TONI MORRISON, *Beloved* (1987)

A MERICANS are obsessed with sex and fearful of black sexuality. The obsession has to do with a search for stimulation and meaning in a fast-paced, market-driven culture; the fear is rooted in visceral feelings about black bodies fueled by sexual myths of black women and men. The dominant myths draw black women and men either as threatening creatures who have the potential for sexual power over whites, or as harmless, desexed underlings of a white culture. There is Jezebel (the seductive temptress), Sapphire (the evil, manipulative bitch), or Aunt Jemima (the sexless, long-suffering nurturer). There is Bigger Thomas (the mad and mean predatory craver of white women), Jack Johnson, the super performer—be it in athletics, entertainment, or sex—who excels others naturally and prefers women of a lighter hue), or Uncle Tom (the spineless, sexless—or is it impotent?—sidekick of whites). The myths offer distorted, dehumanized creatures whose bodies—color of skin, shape of nose and lips, type of hair, size of hips—are already distinguished from the white norm of beauty and whose feared sexual activities are deemed disgusting, dirty, or funky and considered less acceptable.

Yet the paradox of the sexual politics of race in America is that, behind closed doors, the dirty, disgusting, and funky sex associated with black people is often perceived to be more intriguing and interesting, while in public spaces talk about black sexuality is virtually taboo. Everyone knows it is virtually impossible to talk candidly about race without talking about sex. Yet most social

83

scientists who examine race relations do so with little or no reference to how sexual perceptions influence racial matters. My thesis is that black sexuality is a taboo subject in white and black America and that a candid dialogue about black sexuality between and within these communities is requisite for healthy race relations in America.

The major cultural impact of the 1960s was not to demystify black sexuality but rather to make black bodies more accessible to white bodies *on an equal basis*. The history of such access up to that time was primarily one of brutal white rape and ugly white abuse. The Afro-Americanization of white youth—given the disproportionate black role in popular music and athletics—has put white kids in closer contact with their own bodies and facilitated more humane interaction with black people. Listening to Motown records in the sixties or dancing to hip hop music in the nineties may not lead one to question the sexual myths of black women and men, but when white and black kids buy the same billboard hits and laud the same athletic heroes the result is often a shared cultural space where some humane interaction takes place.

This subterranean cultural current of interracial interaction increased during the 1970s and 1980s even as racial polarization deepened on the political front. We miss much of what goes on in the complex development of race relations in America if we focus solely on the racial card played by the Republican Party and overlook the profound multicultural mix of popular culture that has occurred in the past two decades. In fact, one of the reasons Nixon, Reagan, and Bush had to play a racial card, that is, had to code their language about race, rather than simply call a spade a spade, is due to the changed *cultural* climate of race and sex in America. The classic scene of Senator Strom Thurmond—staunch segregationist and longtime opponent of interracial sex and marriage—strongly defending Judge Clarence Thomas—married to a white woman and an alleged avid consumer of white pornography—shows how this change in climate affects even reactionary politicians in America.

Needless to say, many white Americans still view black sexuality with disgust. And some continue to view their own sexuality with disgust. Victorian morality and racist perceptions die hard. But more and more white Americans are willing to interact sexually with black Americans *on an equal basis*—even if the myths still persist. I view this as neither cause for celebration nor reason for lament. Anytime two human beings find genuine pleasure, joy, and love, the stars smile and the universe is enriched. Yet as long as that pleasure, joy, and love is still predicated on myths of black sexuality, the more fundamental challenge of humane interaction remains unmet. Instead, what we have is white access to black bodies on an equal basis—but not yet the demythologizing of black sexuality.

This demythologizing of black sexuality is crucial for black America because much of black self-hatred and self-contempt has to do with the refusal of many black Americans to love their own black bodies—especially their black noses, hips, lips, and hair. Just as many white Americans view black sexuality with disgust, so do many black Americans—but for very different reasons and with very different results. White supremacist ideology is based first and foremost on the degradation of black bodies in order to control them. One of the best ways to instill fear in people is to terrorize them. Yet this fear is best sustained by convincing them that their bodies are ugly, their intellect is inherently underdeveloped, their culture is less civilized, and their future warrants less concern than that of other peoples. Two hundred and forty-four years of slavery and nearly a century of institutionalized terrorism in the form of segregation, lynchings, and second-class citizenship in America were aimed at precisely this devaluation of black people. This white supremacist venture was, in the end, a relative failure—thanks to the courage and creativity of millions of black people and hundreds of exceptional white folk like John Brown, Elijah Lovejoy, Myles Horton, Russell Banks, Anne Braden, and others. Yet this white dehumanizing endeavor has left its toll in the psychic scars and personal wounds now inscribed in the souls of black folk. These scars and wounds are clearly etched on the canvass of black sexuality.

How does one come to accept and affirm a body so despised by one's fellow citizens? What are the ways in which one can rejoice in the intimate moments of black sexuality in a culture that questions the aesthetic beauty of one's body? Can genuine human relationships flourish for black people in a society that assaults black intelligence, black moral character, and black possibility?

These crucial questions were addressed in those black social spaces that affirmed black humanity and warded off white contempt—especially in black families, churches, mosques, schools, fraternities, and sororities. These precious black institutions forged a mighty struggle against the white supremacist bombardment of black people. They empowered black children to learn against the odds and supported damaged black egos so they could keep fighting; they preserved black sanity in an absurd society in which racism ruled unabated; and they provided opportunities for black love to stay alive. But these grand yet flawed black institutions refused to engage one fundamental issue: *black sexuality.* Instead, they ran from it like the plague. And they obsessively condemned those places where black sexuality was flaunted: the streets, the clubs, and the dance-halls.

Why was this so? Primarily because these black institutions put a premium on black survival in America. And black survival required accommodation with and acceptance from white America. Accommodation avoids any sustained association with the subversive and transgressive—be it communism or miscegenation. Did not the courageous yet tragic lives of Paul Robeson and Jack Johnson bear witness to this truth? And acceptance meant that only "good" negroes would thrive—especially those who left black sexuality at the door when they "entered" and "arrived." In short, struggling black institutions made a Faustian pact with white America: avoid any substantive engagement with black sexuality and your survival on the margins of American society is, at least, possible.

White fear of black sexuality is a basic ingredient of white racism. And for whites to admit this deep fear even as they try to instill and sustain fear in blacks is to acknowledge a weakness—a weakness that goes down to the bone. Social scientists have long acknowledged that interracial sex and marriage is the most *perceived* source of white fear of black people—just as the repeated castrations of lynched black men cries out for serious psychocultural explanation.

Black sexuality is a taboo subject in America principally because it is a form of black power over which whites have little control—yet its visible manifestations evoke the most visceral of white responses, be it one of seductive obsession or downright disgust. On the one hand, black sexuality among blacks simply does not include whites, nor does it make them a central point of reference. It proceeds as if whites do not exist, as if whites are invisible and simply don't matter. This form of black sexuality puts black agency center stage with no white presence at all. This can be uncomfortable for white people accustomed to being the custodians of power.

On the other hand, black sexuality between blacks and whites proceeds based on underground desires that Americans deny or ignore in public and over which laws have no effective control. In fact, the dominant sexual myths of black women and men portray whites as being "out of control"—seduced, tempted, overcome, overpowered by black bodies. This form of black sexuality makes white passivity the norm—hardly an acceptable self-image for a white-run society.

Of course, neither scenario fully accounts for the complex elements that determine how any particular relationship involving black sexuality *actually* takes place. Yet they do accent the crucial link between black sexuality and black power in America. In this way, to make black sexuality a taboo subject is to silence talk about a particular kind of power black people are perceived to have over whites. On the surface, this "golden" side is one in which black people simply have an upper hand sexually over whites given the dominant myths in our society.

Yet there is a "brazen" side—a side perceived long ago by black people. If black sexuality is a form of black power in which black agency and white passivity are interlinked, then are not black people simply acting out the very roles to which the racist myths of black sexuality confine them? For example, most black churches shunned the streets, clubs, and dance-halls in part because these black spaces seemed to confirm the very racist myths of black sexuality to be rejected. Only by being "respectable" black folk, they reasoned, would white America see their good works and shed its racist skin. For many black church folk, black agency and white passivity in sexual affairs was neither desirable nor tolerable. It simply permitted black people to play the role of the exotic "other"—closer to nature (removed from intelligence and control) and more prone to be guided by base pleasures and biological impulses.

Is there a way out of this Catch-22 situation in which black sexuality either liberates black people from white control in order to imprison them in racist myths or confines blacks to white "respectability" while they make their own sexuality a taboo subject? There indeed are ways out, but there is no one way out for all black people. Or, to put it another way, the ways out for black men differ vastly from those for black women. Yet, neither black men nor black women can make it out unless both get out since the degradation of both are inseparable though not identical.

Black male sexuality differs from black female sexuality because black men have different self-images and strategies of acquiring power in the patriarchal structures of white America and black communities. Similarly, black male heterosexuality differs from black male homosexuality owing to the self-perceptions and means of gaining power in the homophobic institutions of white America and black communities. The dominant myth of black male sexual prowess makes black men desirable sexual partners in a culture obsessed with sex. In addition, the Afro-Americanization of white youth has been more a male than a female affair given the prominence of male athletes and the cultural weight of male pop artists. This process results in white youth—male and female—imitating and emulating black male styles of walking, talking, dressing, and gesticulating in relation to others. One irony of our present moment is that just as young black men are murdered, maimed, and imprisoned in record numbers, their styles have become disproportionately influential in shaping popular culture. For most young black men, power is acquired by stylizing their bodies over space and time in such a way that their bodies reflect their uniqueness and provoke fear in others. To be "bad" is good not simply because it subverts the language of the dominant white culture but also because it imposes a unique kind of order for young black men on their own distinctive chaos and solicits an attention that makes others pull back with some trepidation. This young black male style is a form of self-identification and resistance in a hostile culture; it also is an instance of machismo identity ready for violent encounters. Yet in a patriarchal society, machismo identity is expected and even exalted—as with Rambo and Reagan. Yet a black machismo style solicits primarily sexual encounters with women and violent encounters with other black men or aggressive police. In this way, the black male search for power often reinforces the myth of black male sexual prowess—a myth that tends to subordinate black and white women as objects of sexual pleasure. This search for power also usually results in a direct confrontation with the order-imposing authorities of the status quo, that is, the police or criminal justice system. The prevailing cultural crisis of many black men is the limited stylistic options of self-image and resistance in a culture obsessed with sex yet fearful of black sexuality.

This situation is even bleaker for most black gay men who reject the major stylistic option of black machismo identity, yet who are marginalized in white America and penalized in black America for doing so. In their efforts to be themselves, they are told they are not really "black men," not machismo-identified. Black gay men are often the brunt of talented black comics like Arsenio Hall and Damon Wayans. Yet behind the laughs lurks a black tragedy of major proportions: the refusal of white and black America to entertain seriously new stylistic options for black men caught in the deadly endeavor of rejecting black machismo identities.

The case of black women is quite different, partly because the dynamics of white and black patriarchy affect them differently and partly because the degradation of black female heterosexuality in America makes black female lesbian sexuality a less frightful jump to make. This does not mean that black lesbians suffer less than black gays—in fact, they suffer more, principally owing to their lower economic status. But this does mean that the subculture of black lesbians is fluid and the boundaries are less policed precisely because black female sexuality in general is more devalued, hence more marginal in white and black America.

The dominant myth of black female sexual prowess constitutes black women as desirable sexual partners—yet the central role of the ideology of white female beauty attenuates the expected conclusion. Instead of black women being the most sought after "objects of sexual pleasure"—as in the case of black men—white women tend to occupy this "upgraded," that is, degraded, position primarily because white beauty plays a weightier role in sexual desirability for women in racist patriarchal America. The ideal of female beauty in this country puts a premium on lightness and softness mythically associated with white women and downplays the rich stylistic manners associated with black women. This operation is not simply more racist to black women than that at work in relation to black men; it also is more devaluing of women in general than that at work in relation to men in general. This means that black women are subject to more multilayered bombardments of racist assaults than black men in addition to the sexist assaults they receive from black men. Needless to say, most black men—especially professional ones—simply recycle this vulgar operation along the axis of lighter hues that results in darker black women bearing more of the brunt than their already devalued lighter sisters. The psychic bouts with self-confidence, the existential agony over genuine desirability, and the social burden of bearing and usually nurturing black children under these circumstances breeds a spiritual strength of black women unbeknownst to most black men and nearly all other Americans.

As long as black sexuality remains a taboo subject, we cannot acknowledge, examine, or engage these tragic psychocultural facts of American life. Furthermore, our refusal to do so limits our ability to confront the overwhelming realities of the AIDS epidemic in America in general and in black America in particular. Although the dynamics of black male sexuality differ from those of black female sexuality, new stylistic options of self-image and resistance can be forged only when black women and men do so together. This is so not because all black people should be heterosexual or with black partners, but rather because all black people—including black children of so-called "mixed" couples—are affected deeply by the prevailing myths of black sexuality. These myths are part of a wider network of white supremacist lies whose authority and legitimacy must be undermined. In the long run, there is simply no way out for all of us other than living out the truths we proclaim about genuine humane interaction in our psychic and sexual lives. Only by living against the grain can we keep alive the possibility that the visceral feelings about black bodies fed by racist myths and promoted by market-driven quests for stimulation do not forever render us obsessed with sexuality and fearful of each other's humanity.

CHAPTER 8

Malcolm X and Black Rage

If ever America undergoes great revolutions, they will be brought about by the presence of the black race on the soil of the United States,—that is to say, they will owe their origin, not to the equality, but to the inequality, of conditions.

ALEXIS DE TOCQUEVILLE,
Democracy in America (1840)

I do not imagine that the white and black races will ever live in any country upon an equal footing. But I believe the difficulty to be still greater in the United States than elsewhere. An isolated individual may surmount the prejudices of religion, of his country, or of his race, and if this individual is a king he may effect surprising changes in society; but a whole people cannot rise, as it were, above itself. A despot who should subject the Americans and their former slaves to the same yoke, might perhaps succeed in commingling their races; but as long as the American democracy remains at the head of affairs, no one will undertake so difficult a task; and it may be foreseen that the freer the white population of the United States becomes, the more isolated will it remain.

ALEXIS DE TOCQUEVILLE,
Democracy in America (1835)

MALCOLM X articulated black rage in a manner unprecedented in American history. His style of communicating this rage bespoke a boiling urgency and an audacious sincerity. The substance of what he said highlighted the chronic refusal of most Americans to acknowledge the sheer absurdity that confronts human beings of African descent in this country—the incessant assaults on black intelligence, beauty, character, and possibility. His profound commitment to affirm black humanity at any cost and his tremendous courage to accent the hypocrisy of American society made Malcolm X the prophet of black rage—then and now.

Malcolm X was the prophet of black rage primarily because of his great love for black people. His love was neither abstract nor ephemeral. Rather, it was a concrete connection with a degraded and devalued people in need of psychic conversion. This is why Malcolm X's articulation of black rage was not directed first and foremost at white America. Rather, Malcolm believed that if black people felt the love that motivated that rage the love would produce a psychic conversion in black people; they would affirm themselves as human beings, no longer viewing their bodies, minds, and souls through white lenses, and believing themselves capable of taking control of their own destinies.

In American society—especially during Malcolm X's life in the 1950s and early 1960s—such a psychic conversion could easily result in death. A proud, self-affirming black person who truly believed in the capacity of black people to throw off the yoke of white racist oppression and control their own destiny usually ended up as one of those strange fruit that Southern trees bore, about which the great Billie Holliday poignantly sang. So when Malcolm X articulated black rage, he knew he also had to exemplify in his own life the courage and sacrifice that any truly self-loving black person needs in order to confront the frightening consequences of being self-loving in American society. In other words, Malcolm X sharply crystallized the relation of black affirmation of self, black desire for freedom, black rage against American society, and the likelihood of early black death.

Malcolm X's notion of psychic conversion holds that black people must no longer view themselves through white lenses. He claims black people will never value themselves as long as they subscribe to a standard of valuation that devalues them. For example, Michael Jackson may rightly wish to be viewed as a person, not a color (neither black nor white), but his facial revisions reveal a self-measurement based on a white yardstick. Hence, despite the fact that he is one of the greatest entertainers who has ever lived, he still views himself, at least in part, through white aesthetic lenses that devalue some of his African characteristics. Needless to say, Michael Jackson's example is but the more honest and visible instance of a rather pervasive self-loathing among many of the black professional class. Malcolm X's call for psychic conversion often strikes horror into this privileged group because so much of who they are and what they do is evaluated in terms of their wealth, status, and prestige in American society. On the other hand, this group often understands Malcolm X's claim more than others precisely because they have lived so intimately in a white world in which the devaluation of black people is so often taken for granted or unconsciously assumed. It is no accident that the black middle class has always had an ambivalent relation to Malcolm X—an open rejection of his militant strategy of wholesale defiance of American society and a secret embrace of his bold truth-telling about the depths of racism in American society. One rarely encounters a picture of Malcolm X (as one does of Martin Luther King, Jr.) in the office of a black professional, but there is no doubt that Malcolm X dangles as the skeleton in the closet lodged in the racial memory of most black professionals.

In short, Malcolm X's notion of psychic conversion is an implicit critique of W. E. B. Du Bois's idea of "double-consciousness." Du Bois wrote:

> The Negro is a sort of seventh son, born with a veil, and gifted with second-sight in this American world,—a world which yields him no true self-consciousness, but only lets him see himself through the revelation of the other world. It is a peculiar sensation, this double-consciousness, this sense of always looking at one's self through the eyes of others, of measuring one's soul by the tape of a world that looks on in amused contempt and pity.

For Malcolm X this "double-consciousness" pertains more to those black people who live "betwixt and between" the black and white worlds—traversing the borders between them yet never settled in either. Hence, they crave peer acceptance in both, receive genuine approval from neither, yet persist in viewing themselves through the lenses of the dominant white society. For Malcolm X, this "double-consciousness" is less a description of a necessary black mode of being in America than a particular kind of colonized mind-set of a special group in black America. Du Bois's "double-consciousness" seems to lock black people into the quest for white approval and disappointment owing mainly to white racist assessment, whereas Malcolm X suggests that this tragic syndrome can be broken through psychic conversion. But how?

Malcolm X does not put forward a direct answer to this question. First, his well-known distinction between "house negroes" (who love and protect the white master) and "field negroes" (who hate and resist the white master) suggests that the masses of black people are more likely to acquire decolonized sensibilities and hence less likely to be "co-opted" by the white status quo. Yet this rhetorical device, though insightful in highlighting different perspectives among black people, fails as a persuasive description of the behavior of "well-to-do" black folk and "poor" black folk. In other words, there are numerous instances of "field negroes" with "house negro" mentalities and "house negroes" with "field negro" mentalities. Malcolm X's often-quoted distinction rightly highlights the propensity among highly assimilated black professionals to put "whiteness" (in all its various forms) on a pedestal, but it also tends to depict "poor" black peoples' notions and enactments of "blackness" in an uncritical manner. Hence his implicit critique of Du Bois's idea of "double-consciousness" contains some truth yet offers an inadequate alternative.

Second, Malcolm X's black nationalist viewpoint claims that the only legitimate response to white supremacist ideology and practice is black self-love and black self-determination free of the tension generated by "double-consciousness." This claim is both subtle and problematic. It is subtle in that every black freedom movement is predicated on an affirmation of African humanity and a quest for black control over the destinies of black people. Yet not every form of black self-love affirms African humanity. Furthermore not every project of black self-determination consists of a serious quest for black control over the destinies of black people. Malcolm's claim is problematic in that it tends to assume that black nationalisms have a monopoly on black self-love and black self-determination. This fallacious assumption confuses the issues highlighted by black nationalisms with the various ways in which black nationalists and others understand these issues.

For example, the grand legacy of Marcus Garvey forces us never to forget that black self-love and black self-respect sit at the center of any possible black freedom movement. Yet this does not mean that we must talk about black self-love and black self-respect in the way in which Garvey did, that is, on an imperial model in which black armies and navies signify black power. Similarly, the tradition of Elijah Muhammad compels us to acknowledge the centrality of black self-regard and black self-esteem, yet that does not entail an acceptance of how Elijah Muhammad talked about achieving this aim, that is, by playing a game of black supremacy that awakens us from our captivity to white supremacy. My point here is that a focus on the issues rightly targeted by black nationalists and an openness to the insights of black nationalists does not necessarily result in an acceptance of black nationalist ideology. Malcolm X tended to make such an unwarranted move—despite his legitimate focus on black self-love, his rich insights on black captivity to white supremacy, and his profound notion of psychic conversion.

MALCOLM X's notion of psychic conversion depends on the idea that black spaces, in which black community, humanity, love, care, concern, and support flourish, will emerge from a boiling black rage. At this point, however, Malcolm X's project falters. How can the boiling black rage be contained and channeled in the black spaces such that destructive and self-destructive consequences are abated? The greatness of Malcolm X is, in part, that he raises this fundamental challenge with a sharpness and urgency never before posed in black America, yet he never had a chance in his short life to grapple with it, nor solve it in idea and deed.

The project of black separatism—to which Malcolm X was beholden for most of his life after his first psychic conversion to the Nation of Islam—suffered from deep intellectual and organizational problems. Unlike Malcolm X's notion of psychic conversion, Elijah Muhammad's idea of religious conversion was predicated on an obsession with white supremacy. The basic aim of black Muslim theology—with its distinct black supremacist account of the origins of white people—was to counter white supremacy. Yet this preoccupation with white supremacy still allowed white people to serve as the principal point of reference. That which fundamentally motivates one still dictates the terms of what one thinks and does—so the motivation of a black supremacist doctrine reveals how obsessed one is with white supremacy. This is understandable in a white racist society—but it is crippling for a despised people struggling for freedom, in that one's eyes should be on the prize, not on the perpetuator of one's oppression. In short, Elijah Muhammad's project remained captive to the supremacy game—a game mastered by the white racists he opposed and imitated with his black supremacy doctrine.

Malcolm X's notion of psychic conversion can be understood and used such that it does not necessarily *entail* black supremacy; it simply rejects black captivity to white supremacist ideology and practice. Hence, as the major black Muslim spokesperson, he had many sympathizers but many fewer Muslim members. Why did Malcolm X permit his notion of psychic conversion to result in black supremacist claims of the Nation of Islam—claims that undermine much of the best of his call for psychic conversion? Malcolm X remained a devoted follower of Elijah Muhammad until 1964 partly because he believed the other major constructive channels of black rage in America—the black church and black music—were less effective in producing and sustaining psychic conversion than the Nation of Islam. He knew that the electoral political system could never address the existential dimension of black rage—hence he, like Elijah, shunned it. Malcolm X also recognized, as do too few black leaders today, that the black encounter with the absurd in racist American society yields a profound spiritual need for human affirmation and recognition. Hence, the centrality of religion and music—those most spiritual of human activities—in black life.

Yet, for Malcolm, much of black religion and black music had misdirected black rage away from white racism and toward another world of heaven and sentimental romance. Needless to say, Malcolm's conception of black Christianity as a white man's religion of pie-in-the-sky and black music as soupy "I Love You B-a-b-y" romance is wrong. While it may be true that most—but not all—of the black music of Malcolm's day shunned black rage, the case of the church-based civil rights movement would seem to counter his charge that black Christianity serves as a sedative to put people to sleep rather than to ignite them to action. Like Elijah Muhammad (and unlike Malcolm X), Martin Luther King, Jr., concluded that black rage was so destructive and self-destructive that without a broad moral vision and political organization, black rage would wreak havoc on black America. His project of nonviolent resistance to white racism was an attempt to channel black rage in political directions that preserved black dignity and changed American society. And his despair at the sight of Watts in 1965 or Detroit and Newark in 1967 left him more and more pessimistic about the moral channeling of black rage in America. To King it looked as if cycles of chaos and destruction loomed on the horizon if these moral channels were ineffective or unappealing to the coming generation. For Malcolm, however, the civil rights movement was not militant enough. It failed to speak clearly and directly to and about black rage.

Malcolm X also seems to have had almost no intellectual interest in dealing with what is distinctive about black religion and black music: *their cultural hybrid character in which the complex mixture of African, European, and Amerindian elements are constitutive of something that is new and black in the modern world.* Like most black nationalists, Malcolm X feared the culturally hybrid character of black life. This fear rested upon the need for Manichean (black/white or male/female) channels for the direction of black rage—forms characterized by charismatic leaders, patriarchal structures, and dogmatic pronouncements. To be sure, these forms are similar to those of other religious organizations around the world, yet the fear of black cultural hybridity among the Nation of Islam is significant for its distinctive form of Manichean theology and authoritarian arrangements. The Manichean theology kept the white world at bay even as it heralded dominant modern European notions like racial supremacy and nationalism. The authoritarian arrangements imposed a top-down disciplined corps of devoted followers who contained their rage in an atmosphere of cultural repression (regulation of clothing worn, books and records consumed, sexual desire, etc.) and paternalistic protection of women.

This complex relation of cultural hybridity and critical sensibility (or jazz and democracy) raises interesting questions. If Malcolm X feared cultural hybridity, to what degree or in what sense was he a serious democrat? Did he believe that the cure to the egregious ills of a racist American "democracy" was more democracy that included black people? Did his relative silence regarding the monarchies he visited in the Middle East bespeak a downplaying of the role of democratic practices in empowering oppressed peoples? Was his fear of cultural hybridity partly rooted in his own reluctance to come to terms with his own personal hybridity, for example, his "redness," light skin, close white friends, etc.?

Malcolm X's fear of cultural hybridity rests upon two political concerns: that cultural hybridity downplayed the vicious character of white supremacy and that cultural hybridity intimately linked the destinies of black and white people such that the possibility of black freedom was farfetched. His fundamental focus on the varieties, subtleties, and cruelties of white racism made him suspicious of any discourse about cultural hybridity. Furthermore, those figures who were most eloquent and illuminating about black cultural hybridity in the 1950s and early 1960s, for example, Ralph Ellison and Albert Murray, were political integrationists. Such a position seemed to pass over too quickly the physical terror and psychic horror of being black in America. To put it bluntly, Malcolm X identified much more with the mind-set of Richard Wright's Bigger Thomas in *Native Son* than with that of Ralph Ellison's protagonist in *Invisible Man*.

Malcolm X's deep pessimism about the capacity and possibility of white Americans to shed their racism led him, ironically, to downplay the past and present bonds between blacks and whites. For if the two groups were, as Martin Luther King, Jr., put it, locked into "one garment of destiny," then the very chances for black freedom were nil. This deep pessimism also rendered Malcolm X ambivalent about American democracy—for if the majority were racist how could the black minority ever be free? Malcolm X's definition of a "nigger" was "a victim of American democracy"— had not the *Herrenvolk* democracy of the United States made black people noncitizens or anticitizens of the Republic? Of course, the aim of a constitutional democracy is to safeguard the rights of the minority and avoid the tyranny of the majority. Yet the concrete practice of the U.S. legal system from 1883 to 1964 promoted a tyranny of the white majority much more than a safeguarding of the rights of black Americans. In fact, these tragic facts drove Malcolm X to look elsewhere for the promotion and protection of black people's rights—to institutions such as the United Nations or the Organization of African Unity. One impulse behind his internationalization of the black freedom struggle in the United States was a deep pessimism about America's will to racial justice, no matter how democratic America was or is.

In addition, Malcolm X's fear of cultural hybridity was linked to his own personal hybridity (he was the grandson of a white man), which blurred the very boundaries so rigidly policed by white supremacist authorities. For Malcolm X, the distinctive feature of American culture was not its cross-cultural syncretism but rather the enforcement of a racial caste system that defined any product of this syncretism as abnormal, alien, and other to both black and white communities. Like Garvey, Malcolm X saw such hybridity, for example, mulattoes, as symbols of weakness and confusion. The very idea of not "fitting in" the U.S. discourse of positively valued whiteness and negatively debased blackness meant one was subject to exclusion and marginalization by whites and blacks. For Malcolm X, in a racist society, this was a form of social death.

One would think that Malcolm X's second conversion, in 1964, to Orthodox Islam might have allayed his fear of cultural hybridity. Yet there seems to be little evidence that he revised his understanding of the radically culturally hybrid character of black life. Furthermore, his deep pessimism toward American democracy continued after his second conversion—though it was no longer based on mythological grounds but solely on the historical experience of Africans in the modern world. It is no accident that the nonblack persons Malcolm X encountered who helped change his mind about the capacity of white people to be human were outside of America and Europe, Muslims in the Middle East. Needless to say, for him, the most striking feature of these Islamic regimes was not their undemocratic practices but rather their acceptance of his black humanity. This great prophet of black rage—with all his brilliance, courage, and conviction—remained blind to basic structures of domination based on class, gender, and sexual orientation in the Middle East.

THE contemporary focus on Malcolm X, especially among black youth, can be understood as both the open articulation of black rage (as in film videos and on tapes targeted at whites, Jews, Koreans, black women, black men, and others) and as a desperate attempt to channel this rage into something more than a marketable commodity for the culture industry. The young black generation are up against forces of death, destruction, and disease unprecedented in the everyday life of black urban people. The raw reality of drugs and guns, despair and decrepitude, generates a raw rage that, among past black spokespersons, only Malcolm X's speech approximates. Yet the issue of psychic conversion, cultural hybridity, black supremacy, authoritarian organization, borders and boundaries in sexuality, and other matters all loom large at present—the same issues Malcolm X left dangling at the end of his short life spent articulating black rage and affirming black humanity.

If we are to build on the best of Malcolm X, we must preserve and expand his notion of psychic conversion that cements networks and groups in which black community, humanity, love, care, and concern can take root and grow (the work of bell hooks is the best example). These spaces—beyond the best of black music and black religion—reject Manichean ideologies and authoritarian arrangements in the name of moral visions, subtle analyses of wealth and power, and concrete strategies of principled coalitions and democratic alliances. These visions, analyses, and strategies never lose sight of black rage, yet they focus this rage where it belongs: on any form of racism, sexism, homophobia, or economic injustice that impedes the opportunities of "everyday people" (to use the memorable phrase of Sly and the Family Stone and Arrested Development) to live lives of dignity and decency. For example, poverty can be as much a target of rage as degraded identity.

Furthermore, the cultural hybrid character of black life leads us to highlight a metaphor alien to Malcolm X's perspective—yet consonant with his performances to audiences—namely, the metaphor of jazz. I use the term "jazz" here not so much as a term for a musical art form, as for a mode of being in the world, an improvisational mode of protean, fluid, and flexible dispositions toward reality suspicious of "either/or" viewpoints, dogmatic pronouncements, or supremacist ideologies. To be a jazz freedom fighter is to attempt to galvanize and energize world-weary people into forms of organization with accountable leadership that promote critical exchange and broad reflection. The interplay of individuality and unity is not one of uniformity and unanimity imposed from above but rather of conflict among diverse groupings that reach a dynamic consensus subject to questioning and criticism. As with a soloist in a jazz quartet, quintet or band, individuality is promoted in order to sustain and increase the *creative* tension with the group—a tension that yields higher levels of performance to achieve the aim of the collective project. This kind of critical and democratic sensibility flies in the face of any policing of borders and boundaries of "blackness," "maleness," "femaleness," or "whiteness." Black people's rage ought to target white supremacy, but also ought to realize that blackness *per se* can encompass feminists like Frederick Douglass or W. E. B. Du Bois. Black people's rage should not overlook homophobia, yet also should acknowledge that heterosexuality *per se* can be associated with so-called "straight" anti-homophobes—just as the struggle against black poverty can be supported by progressive elements of any race, gender, or sexual orientation.

Malcolm X was the first great black spokesperson who looked ferocious white racism in the eye, didn't blink, and lived long enough to tell America the truth about this glaring hypocrisy in a bold and defiant manner. Unlike Elijah Muhammad and Martin Luther King, Jr., he did not live long enough to forge his own distinctive ideas and ways of channeling black rage in constructive channels to change American society. Only if we are as willing as Malcolm X to grow and confront the new challenges posed by the black rage of our day will we take the black freedom struggle to a new and higher level. The future of this country may well depend on it.